Foreword

The game of Cribbage has been around a long, long time and has changed very little along the way. The game is frustratingly simple on the surface, but can prove deceivingly complex upon analysis.

Ever since the game's invention in the early 1630's, a debate has raged concerning averages. In the early years a player of renown named Pasquin, declared the average for two deals was twenty-five points.

Later in the 17th Century, this average was calculated to be twenty-nine. Edmond Hoyle, *the* expert of card games, in the 18th Century debated this number by declaring that twenty-eight was more accurate for a two-deal average.

Old Ed Hoyle has commanded great respect the world over from card players, and to this day most Cribbage experts agree that, indeed, either twenty-eight or twenty-nine is *the* two-deal average.

However, I have made a twenty-year analysis of these numbers, playing and charting thousands of games, and hundreds of thousands of hands. Contrary to old Ed Hoyle and other Cribbage experts, I have found the two-deal average to be 26.4. Compared to a two-deal average of twenty-eight, this projects out to an astonishing 6.4-point difference in eight deals.

One present-day expert, basing his game on the twenty-eight-point average, projects the nondealer of the first hand as the probable winner, winning with two points to spare, after counting first on the ninth deal of an average game.

Another contemporary expert predicts a twenty-nine point two-deal average, with both players standing at 116 after eight average deals, making the game an end-game Pegging toss-up.

But my analysis of the number of deals per game, and of who wins shows that *the dealer, not the non-dealer, wins the majority of nine-deal games.* This analysis is supported by projecting the 26.4 average through nine deals. The nondealer will stand at 115.8 after nine average deals. The dealer, after nine average deals, stands at 121.8 and has won the game.

Using this new 26.4 average as a basis, a method of play slowly evolved—a method I call the "Twenty-six Theory"—that clearly improved my winning average. Journeyman players that I had played for years at a 52-48 average fell at a 55-45 clip when I began using the "Twenty-six Theory."

This book presents a beginning player with the fundamentals, rules, and penalties, and slowly takes him through the basic processes for improving his game. And finally, the chapter "Cribbage for the Expert" describes the controversial "Twenty-six Theory," which should make the journeyman player even better.

But most of all, I hope all of you will be rewarded with as many hours of pleasant companionship and competition with your fellow players as I have had.

DeLynn Colvert

Contents

play winning CRIBBAGE

**written and illustrated by
DeLynn C. Colvert**

Library of Congress Catalog Card Number: 80-67576

Limited Edition - 1980

Published by:
Starr Studios
Warehouse Mall
725 W. Alder
Missoula, MT 59801

Thanks...

A very special thanks to my fellow players. Without their help this book could not have been written. The many pleasant hours of playing Cribbage with them will forever remain a fond memory.

Thanks to Eli Milodragovich (5,053 games), Don Lassila (3,327), Jake "the snake" Tyler (2,010), LaMoure Besse (1,771), Lynn Marsalis (1,714), Ben Lowman (1,029), Randall Herzberg (973), Ted Cote (862), Mary Beth Hartman (708), Bob Knudson (579), Bill Hicks (455), Les Holsapple (223), Darrell Brown (177), Farnum Burbank (174), Ted Putnam (158), John Ross (125), Chuck Bauer (120), Steve Seitz (105), Virginia Braun (104), Orin Kendall (101), Bill Hutcheson (71), Brian Cooper (69), Jim Tour (56), Shannon Johnson (36), Dick Karsky (35), Coard Colvert (30), George Jackson (24), Bob Bjornson (23), Barry Noreen (10), Richard Colvert (10), Alice Burbank (9), Kyle Betz (9), Jim Hill (7), Cindy Junkert (7), Don Weatherhead (7), Jeff Ranf (5), Ernie Amundson (5), Jerry Oltman (5), Jim Oestreich (5), Eric Braun (4), Jack Cooper (2), and Stan Wold (2).

And a special thanks to my dear sister, Lorrie, for giving me my Cribbage board as a high school graduation present.

Cribbidge?. . .No, Cribbage!

SIR JOHN SUCKLING 1609-1642
NODDY AND ONE-AND-THIRTY
POET AND PLAYWRITER
CARD PLAYER AND PLAYBOY
SOLDIER AND POLITICIAN

Cribbidge? . . . No Cribbage!

"Her feet beneath her petticoat
Like little mice, stole in and out,
as if they feared the light,
But O, she dances such a way
No sun upon an Easter-Day
is half so fine a sight."

"Out upon it I have loved
Three whole days together;
And am like to love three more,
If it prove fair weather."

"Why so pale and wan, fond lover?"

These pleasant lyrics were penned by an Englishman in the early 1600's. Almost 400 years ago! Historians claim this Englishman is best remembered for his poetry … his plays … his literary work. But I wonder how many people have read them?

Historians must not be Cribbage players. They must spend their days in musty archives, never enjoying one of life's finer pleasures, wiling away a few moments playing Cribbage.

The author of those lines is Sir John Suckling, and in total disagreement with historians, Sir John's most noted achievement is *not* his literary work. His most noted achievement *is* his invention of Cribbage … that fascinating, exciting, fast-moving card game. Cribbage … that maddening, frustrating, simple card game. A game played by millions the world over, and after nearly 400 years, continues to grow in popularity.

NO! Sir John Suckling is not best known for his literary accomplishments! Without question, Sir John's fame rests with his creation of Cribbage!

Ah, my lads, Cribbage is the game
and no two games are the same
if you be willing
to wager a pound or a shilling
then sit down for a while
and I'll see that your smile
will fade with your ill-fate
when I cut this starter eight
for double pairs royal
'tis sure to make your blood boil
and then a fifteen-two, a fifteen-four
. . .are you asking for more?

The author

SIR JOHN SUCKLING
1609-1642

Who was Sir John Suckling? He was born in England in 1609 into rather comfortable circumstances. His wealthy father was Secretary of State to King James I. Sir John, indeed, was born with a silver spoon in his mouth. *All card players should be so lucky!* His father died while Sir John was a child, and at the age of 18 he inherited a sizable fortune, which he spent freely upon travel, women, and gambling. At 21 he was knighted by King Charles I. Sir John had a gift for words, and his poetry made him a favorite with the King and his Queen. *Actually it was Sir John's card playing ability behind the throne, into the wee hours, that made him a favorite. But he must have taken the King once too often, as Charles shipped him off to war.*

Sir John's military adventures were many. He served under the King of Sweden, Gustavous Adolphus, in Europe, and participated in many sieges ... *out behind the back tents, taking all the raw recruits at "Noddy" and "One-and-Thirty"!*

After the Battle of Leipzig in 1631, in which Gustavous won a brilliant but bloody victory, Sir John returned to England. He was young, rich, and handsome, and back in the King's graces. Sir John soon established a reputation for his wit and his poetry ... and his skill at cards and bowling (according to historians he prized black eyes ... or a lucky hit at bowls ... above his literary achievements). In fact, his skill was such that he was the best card player and best bowler at court.

About this time he invented a new card game. A game he named "Cribbidge." His new game was a variation of "Noddy" and "One-and-Thirty," both popular games at that time. Noddy consisted of markers (or counters), sometimes aided by a "Noddy" board, counting in some fashion to 15 or 21. "One-and-Thirty" was similar, with the number 31 being

the forerunner of the pegging target in Cribbage. *Sir John invented Cribbidge because he was having a terrible run of cards at "Noddy" and was losing his shirt!*

At any rate, his wit, charm, card playing skill, and his fortune carried the day. Cribbidge caught on. It became a favorite among bowlers waiting their turn at the Bowling Green at Piccadilly. The fast-paced, fast-counting game was well suited to the short time between bowling matches.

But not everyone was taken with Sir John's new game. His sisters didn't relish it and reports describe how they came weeping to the Bowling Green to dissuade their brother from playing Cribbidge. They feared he would lose their inheritance. *They needn't have worried. As long as he stayed sober, this was HIS game!*

This life of bowling, card playing, writing, and courting women continued until 1634, when, according to historians, another Sir John (Sir John Digby) gave him a severe beating for making a pass at his fiancee. Sir John Suckling began to "seek more serious society." *Actually, Sir John Suckling pegged double pairs royal twice in the same hand to nip Sir John Digby in the rubber game of a fiercely contested Cribbidge match, cleaning out Digby's wallet. A hardwood Cribbidge board will indeed administer a severe beating!*

In 1635, Sir John (Suckling) was forced to retire to his country estates after Parliament passed a proclamation banning absentee landlordism. Historians report that he thereafter concentrated on writing plays and poetry. *But we all know the true story. The lawmakers, sick and tired of being cleaned out by this sharpie, passed a law to get him out of town. We also know that Sir John didn't concentrate on his poetry, but proceeded to teach the locals this new game of Cribbidge, at the expense of their loose change.*

Civil war between the Scots and the English in 1639 cut short his pleasant country life. Sir John, loyal to good King Charles, joined the fray, supplying 100 troopers on splendidly attired horses. This generous patriotic gesture impressed his peers. *Actually, the troops were in his indebtedness thanks to Cribbidge losses, and his winnings paid for the splendid outfittings.* But Sir John and his troops shared in the Earl of Holland's inglorious retreat before Duns. Poor Sir John was the butt of an amusing ballad, "On Sir John Suckling's Most Warlike Preparations for the Scottish War." *No doubt it was written by one of his many "sore losers."*

But notoriety, good or bad, pays off in politics, and Sir John was elected to Parliament in 1640. Politics proved to be Sir John's undoing, though, as he was implicated in a rescue attempt of Thomas Wentworth, a political prisoner, from the Tower of London. *Thomas was a favorite "pigeon" who kept Sir John in pin money.* The rescue plot was exposed, and Sir John quickly gathered what he could *(three decks of cards and a Cribbidge board)* and fled to France.

Not much was heard from Sir John after that. Rumors had him traveling to Spain with a black-eyed beauty, but the love match didn't last long and he returned to France not long thereafter. *The black-eyed beauty could only speak Spanish, and Sir John was driven to distraction by all that "Cincuenta por dos, cincuenta por cuatro y tres por la seis, siete, y ocho ..."*

The last heard of poor Sir John Suckling is that he committed suicide by poisoning in 1642, after what meager funds he had managed to take to France ran out. *The truth of the matter is he had wagered his entire stake on a game of Cribbidge. Sir John had the game well in hand, having the deal and the Crib hand, needing 2 to make his 121. Sir John pegged only 1! His opponent was 29 points from game, and held the 5 of clubs, the 5 of hearts, the 5 of diamonds, and the Jack of SPADES. The Starter WAS THE 5 OF SPADES! The distraught Sir John promptly drained a vial of poison straightaway!*

See page 22 for explanation

5

Sir John Suckling left a legacy of many plays, poems, and other written works, but of all his accomplishments, his invention of the game of Cribbidge has had the most impact on mankind. As with many words from merry olde England, spellings have changed, usually in simplifying, and Suckling's spelling of "Cribbidge" has evolved into the modern "Cribbage." The game is played by millions the world over. It is especially popular in the United States and the provinces of Canada.

Cribbage is enjoyed by people of all ages. This game—frustratingly simple, yet complex—has grown steadily in popularity. And after some 350 years, its continued growth attests to its sound design, and intriguing play.

Early Cribbage boards were simple hardwood drilled with 60 holes for each player (two rows of 30 holes each) plus a couple of "starter" holes for holding the pegs before the game was under way. Modern Cribbage boards can be found of a great many materials, and in a great variety of shapes and sizes. Boards made from elk and deer antlers, plastic, aluminum, in fact, any material that can be drilled has seemingly been used for Cribbage boards. Huge coffee tables with extra large pegs are commonly found, as are small miniature boards.

A game can be joined almost any place two people can get together. Travelers find Cribbage an excellent way to pass a long, monotonous trip. Aunts and uncles play with nephews and nieces, grandparents with grandchildren, fathers and mothers with sons and daughters. And in this book, you will be playing with Uncle Jake, "the snake."

Uncle Jake is a sharpie of my acquaintance, who would have given Sir John a run for his money. To learn to play Cribbage like a pro you must play with a pro, and that's where "the snake" comes in. He'll show up when we get the cards out.

Today, as in Sir John's time, Cribbage and gambling go hand in hand. Many Cribbage players feel it's a waste of time if there isn't something on the game. Sam Clemens—Mark Twain to most of us—wrote about this sentiment in "The 1,000,000 Pound Bank Note":

After refreshments, tables were brought, and we all played Cribbage, six pence a game. The English never play any game for amusement. If they can't make something—or lose something, they don't care which—they won't play.

No doubt about it, gambling adds a little zest to any game, whether for a few pennies or a few dollars. That's why Cribbage tournaments abound in local clubs and bars where the stakes range from "a nickel a point" up to amounts that would have frightened Sir John's sisters.

But let's get back to the basics before we start wagering.

Sir John's game of "Cribbidge" was played with five cards, with variations of the game evolving into a six-card game. Edmund Hoyle, the 18th century Whist instructor who became famous for his book of game rules ("According to Hoyle"), had this to say about six-card Cribbage:

This game is also played with the whole pack, but both in skill and scientific arrangement it is vastly inferior to that played with five cards. Still it is a pleasant resource in a dull hour, and abounds with amusing points and combinations without taxing the mind much ...

Perhaps modern man has become lazy, or perhaps old Ed Hoyle didn't know as much as he thought he did, for six-card Cribbage became the most popular, and now the six-card game is THE GAME!

Enough talk, let's get out the Cribbage board and cards!

Beginning Cribbage

Beginning Cribbage

Cribbage, like most card games, is a numbers game. Four of this, and four of that, thirteen of this and thirteen of that . . . and fifty-two in all. Fifty-two cards dealt in combinations of six (each player receives six cards in two-handed Cribbage) can reach millions of combinations (one Cribbage expert places the number at 936,491,920 possible combinations). When these millions of combinations are coupled with a playing board on which the first player to score 121 points is the winner, it's clear, Cribbage is, indeed, a numbers game!

Lord Kelvin, a famous 19th century physicist, could have had Cribbage in mind when he wrote:

I often say that when you can measure what you are speaking about, and express it in numbers, you know something about it; but when you cannot express it in numbers, your knowledge is of a meager and unsatisfactory kind.

This book teaches you those numbers. This book teaches you to be a winner.

Yes, you must have an aptitude for numbers to become a first-class Cribbage player, a winning player. But to thoroughly enjoy the game, you needn't be an Albert Einstein, and anyone can master the fundamentals with just a few minutes of study.

First, you must have a standard pack of fifty-two playing cards (no Jokers, please). Cards are ranked from the Ace (low) through the King (high). Cards carry their face value: a 7-card is valued at seven, a 6-card at six, and so forth. An Ace is worth one, while a 10-card, Jack, Queen, or King counts ten.

Cards that have face value

Cards with a value of ten

9

Second, you need a scoring board. Many types of Cribbage boards are sold, but for reasons described later in the book, buy a board that has two tracks of 120 holes, plus two starting holes and a winner's hole (hole 121). Such a board eliminates errors and confusion that accompany the boards with sixty holes that require two trips around to complete the 121-point game.

The board should have easily distinguishable holes, preferably numbered (5, 10, 15, etc.), or at least a board that has holes spaced to make counting easy. It is imperative to know where you and your opponent are on the board at a glance. This is not too important when learning the game, but becomes critical as your skill increases.

Pegs are used to keep track of points scored. Each player has two pegs, preferably of a different color than his opponent. When a player scores his first point or points of the game, he inserts a peg into the correct hole. For example, a player scores two points to start the game, promptly inserting a peg into the second hole. He then scores three more points, and uses his other peg to "leapfrog" the first peg, placing it in the fifth hole. This "leapfrogging" method of pegging allows your opponent to check your score and insures accurate scoring. After scoring two points to start the game, and three points with your second score, your pegs should be in the second and fifth holes. Your opponent can easily see you scored three points with your last score.

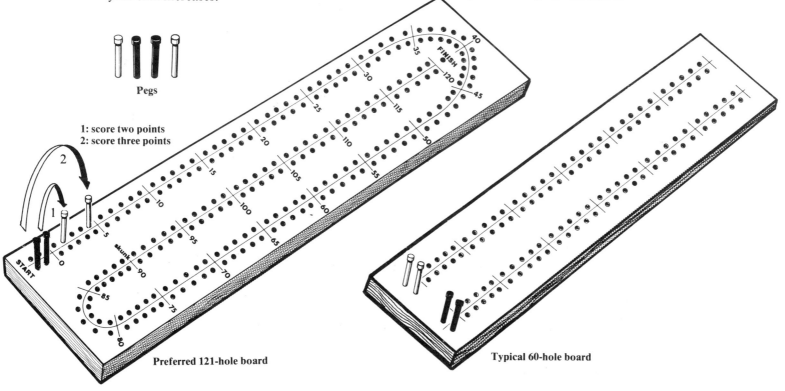

Pegs

1: score two points
2: score three points

Preferred 121-hole board

Typical 60-hole board

How are points scored? First a dealer is established and six cards are dealt to each player. Both players discard two cards to form an extra hand called the "Crib." This Crib hand is the property of the dealer. After discarding, the deck is cut and the top card of the cut deck is turned face up. This is the "Starter" card. Each hand is then played, with the nondealer playing the first card. Play then alternates between players. Points scored (and pegged) with this interplay is called "Pegging." After Pegging is completed, the nondealer counts his hand (in combination with the Starter card) and marks his progress on the board with *his* pegs. *After* the nondealer counts his hand, the dealer counts his hand (in combination with the Starter card), using *his* pegs to mark his progress. Finally, the dealer counts his Crib hand (again in combination with the Starter card), completing the play of the hand. The nondealer then shuffles and redeals, with dealing alternating until 121 points and game are reached. Combinations that score in Pegging and counting of the hands are described later, but first, let's go through the game, step by step.

To begin play, each player cuts the deck. The player cutting the lowest card (remember, the Ace is low) deals. The player who cuts first should be a gentleman (or a lady) and leave about half the deck for the other player to cut. Also, according to old Ed Hoyle, you must cut at least four cards deep.

The player cutting the Ace has won the deal

The dealer shuffles the cards (the nondealer can demand to shuffle first, but this option rarely is exercised) and he deals six cards, one at a time, face down, alternating between players. Because Cribbage is a "Gentleman's" game, there is no cut after the shuffle.

The two players then pick up their six cards. Each discards two cards face down to the "Crib"—forming an extra hand to be counted and scored by the dealer (*after* the hands have been counted).

After the "Crib" hand has been formed, the nondealer cuts the deck. The dealer turns the top card of the cut deck face up. This card is called the "Starter" card. If the Starter card is a Jack, the dealer promptly announces "two for the Jack" and pegs two points on the Cribbage board.

Now we are ready to begin play, called "Pegging." Remember, the cards are counted at face value (the Ace valued at one, the King at ten, etc.). First, let's identify the combinations of cards that score points in Pegging:

Scoring In Pegging

- Cutting the Jack as Starter card: dealer scores two points

- Pair: two points

- Three of a kind (pairs royal): six points

- Four of a kind (double pairs royal): 12 points

- Run (or sequence): one point for each card in the run (minimum of three)

- Running count totaling fifteen: two points

- "Go" (under thirty-one): one point

- "Thirty-one" (exactly): two points

In pegging, the nondealer plays first, then the dealer, with play then alternating between them. Counting cards at their face value, the count continues to go higher with each card played. The object or target is "thirty-one." If thirty-one cannot be scored exactly, the player who played last gets a "Go" and pegs one point. If he reaches thirty-one, he pegs two points. The count cannot exceed thirty-one. If a player is stymied and cannot play further, he announces "Go." His opponent continues to play his cards, if possible. His goal is thirty-one. If he reaches it, he collects two points; if not he collects one point for the "Go." Pegging resumes with the remaining cards in the hand and play alternates. If your opponent played the last card and received the "Go," it is your turn to begin a new sequence to thirty-one.

Let's go through a few examples of Pegging. The nondealer begins play by choosing a card from his hand and laying it down in front of himself face up and announcing its value. For example, if it is the 4 of diamonds, he announces "four" (suits are not announced in Pegging). The dealer responds by lay-ing down another 4 in front of himself (the dealer and nondealer keep their hands separated) and says, "eight, and two for the pair" and promptly pegs two points. The nondealer continues play by laying a 7, saying "fifteen . . . two" (meaning the count is at fifteen and he pegs two points for the fifteen). The dealer plays a Jack and says, "twenty-five." The nondealer follows with a five and exclaims "thirty." The dealer doesn't have an Ace and says "Go." The nondealer, also without an Ace, pegs his one point for the "Go."

Now the dealer starts a new sequence to thirty-one. The dealer plays a King, announcing "ten"; the non-dealer follows with his last card, a Jack, saying "twenty," and the dealer follows with his last card, luckily a Queen, to form a run of three, and says "thirty, a run of three and one for last card" and pegs four holes.

Reviewing this hand, the nondealer scored three points (two for the fifteen, one for the "Go"). The dealer scored six points (two for the pair of 4's, three for the run of the Jack, Queen, King, and one for the last card).

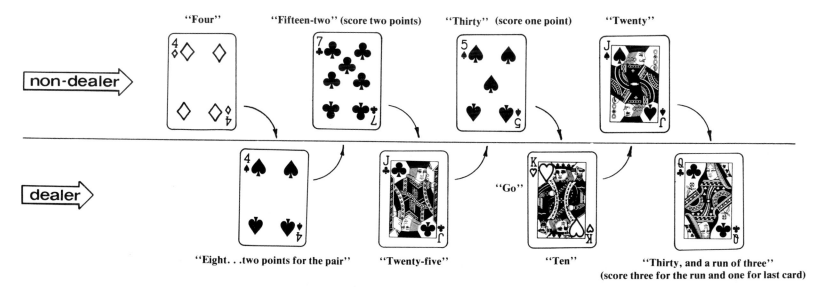

"Four" "Fifteen-two" (score two points) "Thirty" (score one point) "Twenty"

non-dealer

dealer

"Eight. . .two points for the pair" "Twenty-five" "Go" "Ten" "Thirty, and a run of three"
(score three for the run and one for last card)

Let's peg a few sample hands to get the feel of the process:

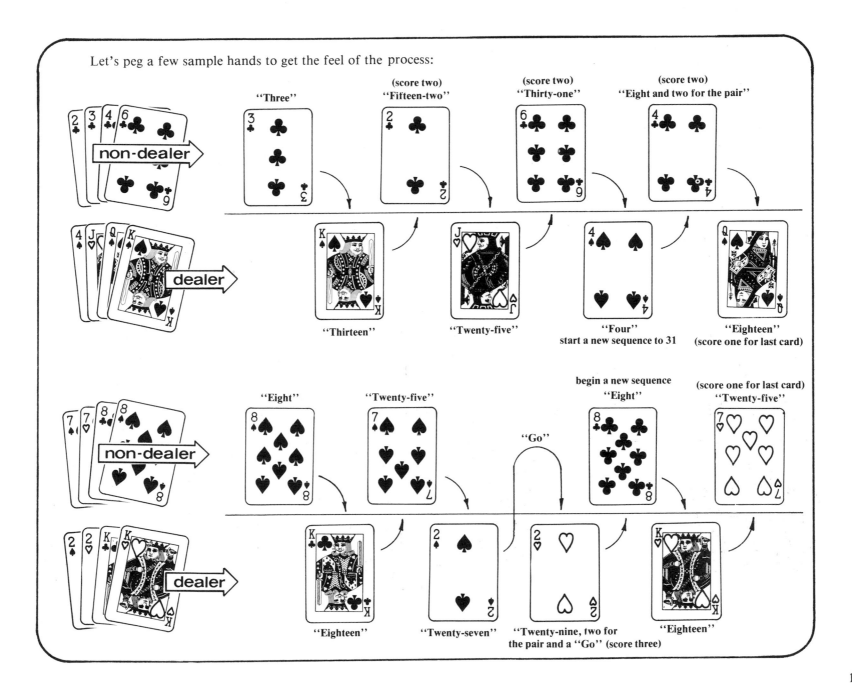

"Three"

(score two)
"Fifteen-two"

(score two)
"Thirty-one"

(score two)
"Eight and two for the pair"

"Thirteen"

"Twenty-five"

"Four"
start a new sequence to 31

"Eighteen"
(score one for last card)

"Eight"

"Twenty-five"

"Go"

begin a new sequence
"Eight"

(score one for last card)
"Twenty-five"

"Eighteen"

"Twenty-seven"

"Twenty-nine, two for
the pair and a "Go" (score three)

"Eighteen"

The run in Pegging is three (or more) cards that form a numerical run. They need *not* be played in order, but must form a sequence uninterrupted by any "foreign" card. Your opponent's card, combined with your cards, form runs. In case of a "Go," you may play out your remaining cards to form a run, and your opponent may do likewise. A run *cannot* be continued after thirty-one has been reached. One point is scored for each card in the run. A three-card run is three points, a four-card run is four points, and so on. The longest run possible in Pegging is a seven-point run (Ace-2-3-4-5-6-7). This peg count is twenty-eight, making the 8-card impossible to add to the run.

The key question when a run's legitimacy is in doubt is, "Do the cards form a sequence, no matter what order played?" For example, the peg is as follows: 7, 9, 8 (score a run of three), then a 6 is added (score a run of four). The count is at thirty and is a "Go." No further cards may be played on this run. The count begins again. Another example: 5, 3, 2, 4 (score a run of four), Ace (score a run of five and two points for the total peg score of fifteen—seven points in all), 6 (score a run of six). A run may be formed back to back with another run. An example: 4, 3, 5 (score a run of three), then a 4, using the previous two cards (3 and 5) to form another run scoring three points. Let's go through a few more examples:

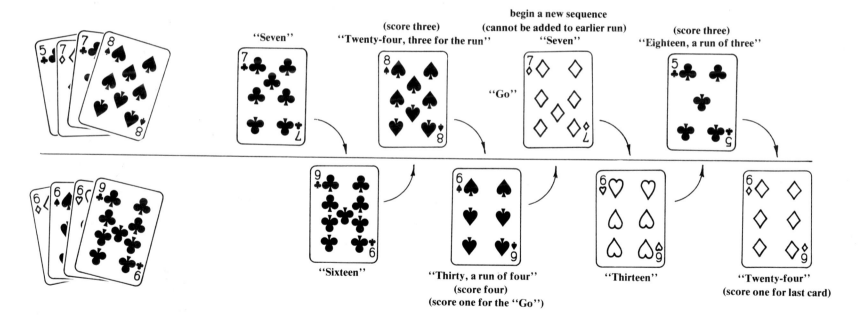

14

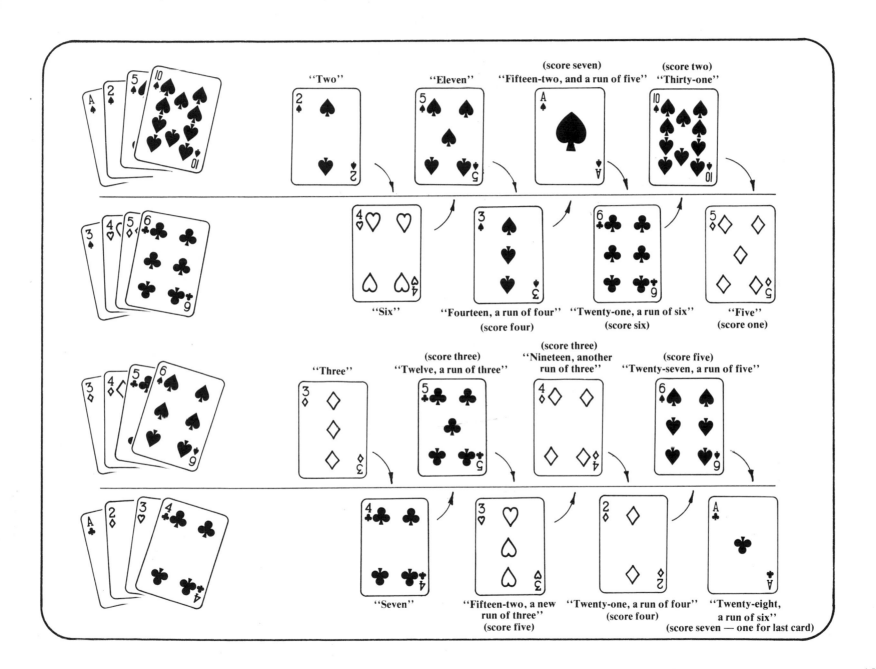

"Two"   "Eleven"   (score seven)
"Fifteen-two, and a run of five"   (score two)
"Thirty-one"

"Six"   "Fourteen, a run of four"   "Twenty-one, a run of six"   "Five"
(score four)   (score six)   (score one)

"Three"   (score three)
"Twelve, a run of three"   (score three)
"Nineteen, another run of three"   (score five)
"Twenty-seven, a run of five"

"Seven"   "Fifteen-two, a new run of three"   "Twenty-one, a run of four"   "Twenty-eight, a run of six"
(score five)   (score four)   (score seven — one for last card)

15

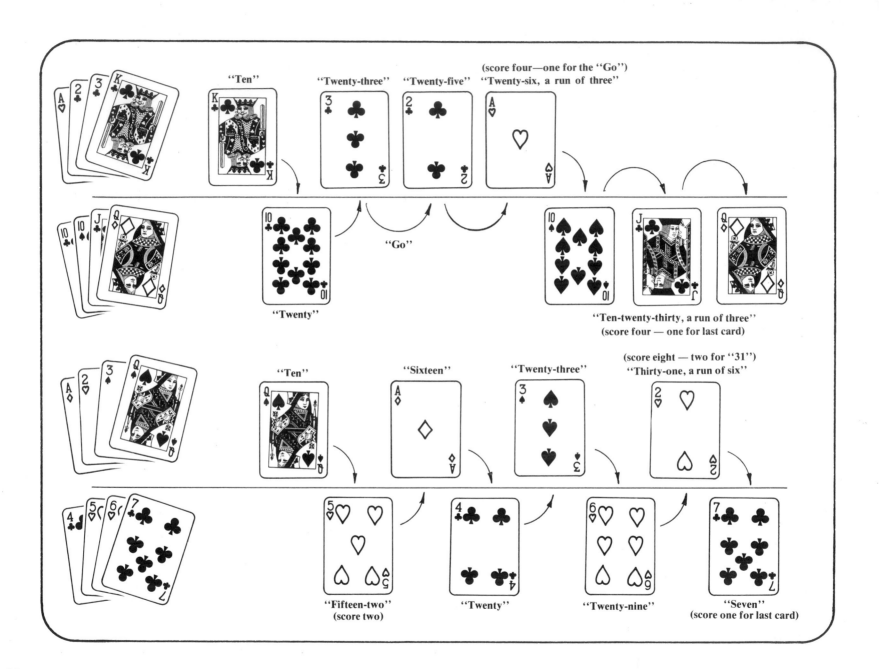

"Ten"

"Twenty-three" "Twenty-five"

(score four—one for the "Go")
"Twenty-six, a run of three"

"Twenty"

"Go"

"Ten-twenty-thirty, a run of three"
(score four — one for last card)

"Ten"

"Sixteen"

"Twenty-three"

(score eight — two for "31")
"Thirty-one, a run of six"

"Fifteen-two"
(score two)

"Twenty"

"Twenty-nine"

"Seven"
(score one for last card)

Scoring The Hands And Crib

Pegging is completed when all eight cards of the two hands have been played. After Pegging is completed, the hands and the Crib are counted. The nondealer counts his hand *first*. This is the great equalizer in Cribbage, as the dealer counts two hands (his hand and his Crib) and would have a great advantage at the end of the game if both the dealer and nondealer counted simultaneously. If the nondealer reaches "game" (121 points), the dealer cannot count his hand or the Crib, and has lost the game.

Card combinations that score are basically the same as in Pegging, except the Starter card becomes a fifth card in the hands and the Crib. In addition, flushes (cards of the same suit) now have value. Pairs count two; three-of-a-kind, is six; four-of-a-kind, twelve; runs (three or more) are valued at one for each card in the run. Cards totaling fifteen score two points. The Jack, if it is the same suit as the Starter card, is one point. Sir John named this special Jack "Nobs." A flush (all four cards in the hand are the same suit) is worth four points. If the Starter card is also of the same suit, the flush bonus is worth five points. The Crib, however, *cannot score a four-card flush. The Crib must have all five cards of the same suit to count the five-point bonus.*

In addition, any run that has *different* combinations of cards may be counted.

This same rule applies to combinations that add to fifteen. Any *different* combination of cards totaling fifteen scores two points.

Pair: two points

Three of a kind: six points

Four of a Kind: twelve points

Three-card run: three points

Four-card run: four points

Jack same suit as Starter card: one point

Five-card run: five points

 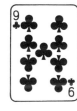 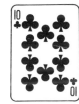 

Four-card flush (hand only): four points
(Starter card another suit)

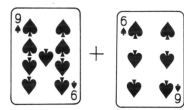

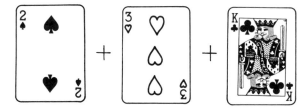

Any combination of fifteen: two points

Five-card flush (hand and Crib): five points

Now, let's have some examples of scoring the TOTAL HAND:

Starter + Hand

"Fifteen-two's"

 + = 2

 + = 2

 + = 2

 +  + +  = 4

Single run of four

Nobs  = 1

———
11

A Double Run:

  **A Double Run of three is *always* eight points, *plus* fifteen's, flushes, and Nobs** = **8**

"Fifteen-two"  +  = **2**

"Fifteen-two" + = **2**

12

 **A Double Run of four is *always* ten points, *plus* fifteen's, flushes, and Nobs** **10**

10

A Triple Run:

  **A Triple Run is *always* fifteen points, *plus* fifteen's, flushes, and Nobs** = **15**

"Fifteen-two"  = **2**

_____

17

A Quadruple Run:

 **A Quadruple Run is *always* sixteen points, *plus* fifteen's, flushes, and Nobs** = **16**

Nobs  = **1**

_____

17

The most miscounted hand in Cribbage:

 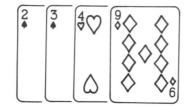 **9**

The next two most miscounted hands:

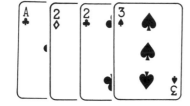 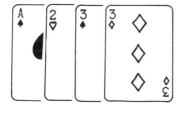 **14**

  **14**

The perfect hand:

 **29**

  **24**

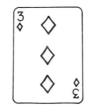  **24**

  **24**

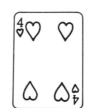  **24**

  **23**

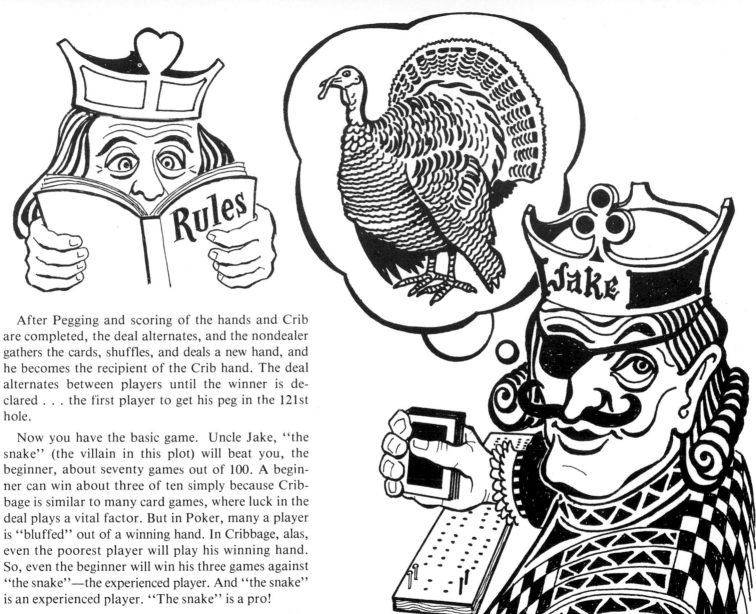

After Pegging and scoring of the hands and Crib are completed, the deal alternates, and the nondealer gathers the cards, shuffles, and deals a new hand, and he becomes the recipient of the Crib hand. The deal alternates between players until the winner is declared . . . the first player to get his peg in the 121st hole.

Now you have the basic game. Uncle Jake, "the snake" (the villain in this plot) will beat you, the beginner, about seventy games out of 100. A beginner can win about three of ten simply because Cribbage is similar to many card games, where luck in the deal plays a vital factor. But in Poker, many a player is "bluffed" out of a winning hand. In Cribbage, alas, even the poorest player will play his winning hand. So, even the beginner will win his three games against "the snake"—the experienced player. And "the snake" is an experienced player. "The snake" is a pro!

Before going further, we must have some guidelines . . . some rules to follow. Rules to keep "the snake" in line!

23

Cribbage Rules

1. Before beginning a game, players must agree on:
   - Whether the game will be sixty-one or 121 points.
   - Whether a skunk (or lurch) will count a double game (in a sixty-one-point game, scoring thirty points or less is a skunk; in a 121-point game, scoring ninety points or less is a skunk).
   - Whether a double skunk (or double lurch) scores as four games. This occurs in a 121-point game only. A player is double skunked if he scores sixty points or less.
   - Whether "Muggins" will be in effect. "Muggins" entitles a player to take for himself any points overlooked by his opponent (in Pegging, hand, or Crib). "Muggins" is declared after your opponent has removed his fingers from his peg, or when Pegging, after he declares the count, and fails to call his points.

2. To establish the first dealer, each player cuts the deck. The low card wins the deal. In case of a tie, cut again. (Option: high card deals.) The player who cuts first must cut at least four cards deep, leaving at least half the deck for the other player.

3. The nondealer may shuffle the deck, but the dealer has the right to the last shuffle.

4. The deck is not cut before dealing (Option: local rules, or the players may agree to allow a cut).

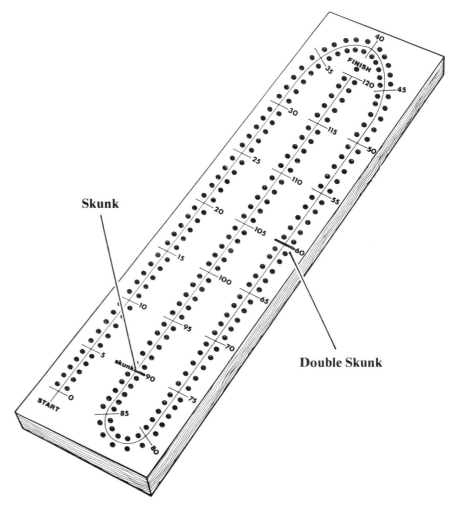

Skunk

Double Skunk

5. Cards are dealt one by one, starting with the non-dealer, and alternating between players until six are dealt to each player.

6. Cards must not be touched until the deal is completed.

7. The nondealer discards two cards face down to the Crib hand; then the dealer does likewise. The Crib hand belongs to the dealer, to be counted at a later time.

8. Cards once discarded to the Crib cannot be picked up for reconsideration.

9. The Crib, once formed, may be touched only by the dealer, but only *after* counting his hand.

10. The nondealer cuts the deck for the Starter card. He must cut at least three cards deep and leave a minimum of four cards. The dealer turns up the Starter card.

11. If the Starter card is a Jack, the dealer is entitled to two points, which must be pegged *before* he plays a card (the dealer can *still* claim his two points after the nondealer has played his first card, however).

12. The nondealer *always* plays the first card in Pegging.

13. A card legally played in Pegging cannot be recalled.

14. If a card is *not legally played* in Pegging, it can be recalled without penalty.

15. After removing your fingers from the peg, the score cannot be changed (your opponent may claim "Muggins," however, if you have agreed to that option).

16. There is no penalty if a mistake is made in adding to thirty-one. However, the error must be corrected upon demand of the opponent before another card is played. Thereafter, the error cannot be corrected.

17. Each player determines his count. No help can be asked for from his opponent or from spectators.

18. The hands of both players and Crib must be exposed to the opponent until he agrees to the count being claimed.

19. Once the hand or Crib has been counted and pegged, and the fingers removed from the peg, any unclaimed points are forfeited. In the case of a declared blank hand or Crib, after the cards are picked up for a new deal, any unclaimed points are forfeited.

20. Spectators shall not interfere in any way with the game.

Misdealing and Penalties

Some irregularities incur no penalties. Other irregularities are penalized. These rules pertain to misdealing and are *not* penalized:

- The dealer exposes one (or more) of *his* cards. The nondealer has the option of calling for a new deal *if* he has *not* looked at his own cards.

- The nondealer exposes one (or more) of his cards. The dealer has the option of redealing, provided he has *not* looked at his cards.

- The nondealer is dealt *more* than six cards, but does not discover the error until *after* he picks up his cards: redeal.

- The dealer discovers he has given himself more than six cards. The nondealer has the option of drawing the excess card or cards from the hand and putting them on top of the deck, *or* the nondealer may demand a new deal.

- Either player is dealt fewer than six cards: redeal.

- The cards are not dealt one at a time: redeal.

- The deck contains a card or cards that are face up: redeal.

Some irregularities incur a penalty during play, including several for misdealing. These rules cover irregularities that *are* penalized:

- The dealer exposed a nondealer's card when dealing: the nondealer scores two points and may demand a new deal (provided the nondealer has *not* looked at his other cards).

- The nondealer discovers more than six cards dealt to him *before* picking them up: the nondealer scores a two-point penalty. Redeal.

- After the cards are picked up, either player finds his opponent with an improper number of cards in his hand or Crib: two-point penalty. Redeal. Option: the dealer adds card or cards from top of deck to short hand, or either opponent draws any extras from hand and places them on top of deck. Penalty remains two points.

- Either player touches the deck *before* cutting for the "Starter" card (after the deal has been completed and the deck placed aside): Offending player forfeits two points.

- Either player confuses his cards with the Crib hand: two-point penalty. Redeal.

- A player announces "Go" and neglects to play a card when he could count to thirty-one, or under: two-point penalty.

- Either player pegs more points than he is entitled: his opponent demands he correct the score and claims the number of over-scored points to his score as a penalty.

- A player fails to peg entitled points: forfeiture of overlooked points *after* playing *his* next card.

- Touching an opponent's peg: two-point penalty.

- Touching your pegs without being entitled to score: two-point penalty.

- A player removes his opponent's front peg: his opponent may claim a forfeited game.

- A player accidentally displaces his front peg: place peg in hole behind back peg, or replace it, with opponent's consent, to correct hole.

- One player dislodges pegs by accident: other player replaces pegs in proper place (if refused, game is forfeited by player who dislodged pegs).

- Both players dislodge pegs by accident: pegs are replaced by mutual agreement, or game is voided.

- A player fails to peg for his hand or Crib *before* returning cards to dealer for the next deal: forfeiture of entitled points.

- Either player refuses to pay a penalty by infringing the rules: forfeiture of game.

Beginning Play

Now you have the rules and the basic information to play the game. But how do you play the game? What is the strategy? How do you win consistently? No one wants to win only three of ten. Without basic strategy, playing each hand blindly, the beginner will be mired in a 30% rut. Old Uncle Jake will relentlessly win his 70%. If you are a beginner . . . and a wagering man (one of those Englishmen Samuel Clemens wrote about), you should not play a seasoned player for any loose change . . . unless you get 2 to 1 odds, and then *only* if you have won the first deal. Skill levels being equal, the first dealer will win about 12% more games than his opponent. Playing against a skilled player, this 12% edge, with a 2 to 1 bet, will make you a winner of the loose change.

But no one wants to be given such an edge . . . it's bad for the ego! So, on with learning the game!

Recognizing Good Hands

First, a player must recognize what constitutes a good hand. Study the diagrams. They show the type of hands that pile up the score. Holding double runs that also combine into combinations of fifteen will make Uncle Jake sweat. For example, runs of 4, 5, 6, 6, 7, 8, and 7, 8, 9 have combinations that add to fifteen. Ten-cards (10, Jack, Queen, and King) combined with the 5-card add to fifteen, and are easy to help with the Starter card (the deck contains sixteen 10-cards and four 5-cards—roughly 40% of the deck). Also, small card combinations adding to five (Ace-4, 2-3) are easily helped by the sixteen 10-cards.

Recognizing good hands comes with practice. Learn to recognize which four cards of the six will score maximum count with the "right" Starter card. Many times you will want to keep the very best count possible, regardless of the odds of cutting the Starter card you need for maximum count. Play a few games at a leisurely pace and this knack of recognizing hands will come naturally. Secondly, study the rules. Many games are decided by a single point. An error, a missed count, or a single two-point penalty can be fatal. Especially so, if you have agreed to play "Muggins."

Examples of hand recognition (for maximum count):

Discard the 4-Queen. A 2 Starter card will score fourteen points

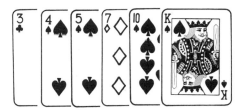

Discard the 10-King. A 3 Starter card will score fourteen points

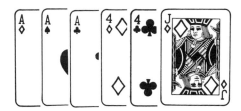

Discard the 4 of diamonds-Jack to your Crib, the 4 of clubs-Jack to Jake's Crib. Any "ten" card or 9 will score twelve points

Discard the 3-King. A 5 of spades Starter card will score thirteen points

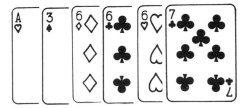

Discard the Ace-7. A 3 Starter card will score twenty points (and a 9 will score eighteen)

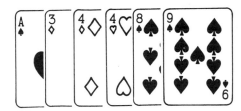

Discard the Ace-9. A 2, 5, or 8 Starter card will score twelve points. A 4-starter card will score fourteen points.

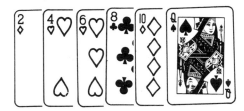

Discard the 2-8. A 5 Starter card will score nine points. However, the 2-4-6-8 combination is a better pegging hand—check the board.

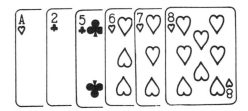

Discard the 2-5. Keep the flush. A 7 or 8 Starter card will score twenty points

Discard the 9-10. The 5 of hearts Starter card will score twenty-three points. Any "Ten" card will score sixteen (The Jack Starter would score twenty points)

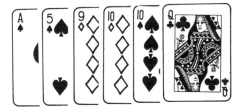

Discard the Ace-9 if playing for absolute maximum. A Jack or 5 Starter card would score sixteen; however, the 5-9-10-10 combination would score fourteen with a Jack Starter, *and* gives you the opportunity for a twelve hand with an 8 Starter card. Check the board.

Discarding To The Crib

After studying your six-card hand, the next question is: what two cards to discard to the Crib hand? But first: Whose Crib is it? If it's your Crib, you want to lay away good cards—cards that will be the foundation (you hope) of a strong, high counting hand. As Jake "the snake" would say when he deals, "I salted the Crib, old buddy, look out!"

So, if it's your Crib, salt away. But do *not* destroy a good hand in the process. The bulk of your score will come from the hand, *not* the Crib. It's much easier to draw one card—the Starter card—to *four* known cards (your hand) than it is to draw to *two* known cards (your Crib discard) and your opponent's *two unknown* discards. At times your hand will contain only two matching cards, with little hope of forming a good hand, regardless of the Starter card. In this case, lay away the two matching cards in *your* Crib in hopes of scoring at least a good Crib hand.

When the Crib hand belongs to your opponent, your goal is to stymie the Crib, to balk the Crib . . . to make the Crib as worthless as possible. Pairs, cards closely related that could form a run of three (or even four), cards that add to fifteen, and especially the 5-card, should *not* be discarded to your opponent's Crib. Good discards to balk a Crib are combinations such as a King-10, King-9, Queen-8, or other combinations that cannot possibly add to fifteen or make a three-card run.

The King is the very best discard to an opponent's Crib, as the odds of it being used in a run are less than other cards (except the Ace). The reason is because the King is the end card of the run, cutting the chance of its being used in a three-card run a full 33% over a Queen, and 50% over the Jack, 10, 9, 8, 7, 6, 5, 4, and 3.

To clarify these odds, the King combines with *only* the Queen and Jack to form a three-card run. There are four Queens and four Jacks—eight cards. But the Queen can combine with the King, Jack, and 10 to form a three-card run—twelve cards. The Jack combines with the King, Queen, 10, and 9 to form a three-card run—sixteen cards. Sixteen cards also combine with the 10, 9, 8, 7, 6, 5, 4, and 3 to form three-card runs. Again, the Ace is also the end card of the sequence of thirteen, allowing only eight cards to form a three-card run. The Deuce can be combined with twelve cards to form a three-card run. But the Ace and Deuce are not as good to discard as the King and Queen because the Ace and Deuce can be combined with *any* card in the deck to form 15's. For example: A-4-K, 1-6-8, A-9-5, 2-3-J, 2-6-7, 2-8-5. In addition, the Ace and Deuce are valuable cards in Pegging, for forming runs, 15's, and getting "Go."

There will be times—agonizing times—when a decision must be made whether you should destroy your hand to balk your opponent's Crib. These decisions come with experience. Board position determines your decision in many of these tough situations. Later in the book, we'll analyze board position and strategy, but let's get the basics first.

In discarding to your opponent's Crib, it is impossible to completely balk his Crib. All you can do is *cut down* his odds of getting a good one. Any discard has the potential of at least fourteen points. For example, you discard the King-9. Your opponent discards a pair of 5's, and the Starter card is a 5—a fourteen-point Crib hand! A longshot, but possible. Avoid discards that have a higher potential—especially those forming hands of twenty or more (7-8 or 4-6, for example).

The odds of cards forming 3-card runs:

   8

The King combines with four Queens, four Jacks

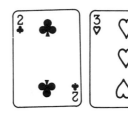 8

The Ace combines with four 2's, four 3's

  12

The Queen combines with four Kings, four Jacks, and four 10's

 12

The 2 combines with four Aces, four 3's, and four 4's

 16

The Jack combines with four Kings, four Queens, four 10's, and four 9's

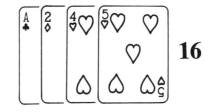 16

The 3 combines with four Aces, four 2's, four 4's, and four 5's

The 4,5,6,7,8,9, and 10 also combine with sixteen cards to form a 3-card run

In summary, when the Crib is yours, discard cards that could be the foundation of a good hand . . . salt away good combinations. When the Crib belongs to your opponent, discard dissimilar cards, cards that will *not* combine into a high counting hand . . . balking cards! Study the diagrams for discarding to the Crib. The basic process is simple, and with a little thought, you will quickly acquire good basic discarding ability.

Your Crib: Discard the 7-8
Jake's Crib: Discard the Ace-Queen

Discarding to the Crib:

Your Crib: discard to 9-10
Jake's Crib: discard the 10-King

Your Crib: discard the Queens
Jake's Crib: discard the 3-Queen of clubs

Your Crib: discard the Jack-Queen
Jake's Crib: discard the 10-Queen

Your Crib: discard the 8-9
Jake's Crib: discard the 9-King

Your Crib: discard the 2-10 (flush try)
Jake's Crib: discard the 2-King

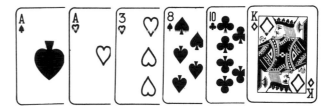

Your Crib: discard the 8-10
Jake's Crib: discard the 8-King

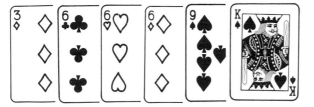

Your Crib: discard the 3-King
Jake's Crib: discard the 9-King

Your Crib: discard the 5-10
Jake's Crib: discard the 10-King of diamonds

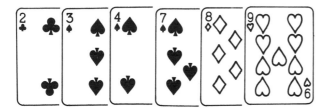

Your Crib: discard the 7-8
Jake's Crib: discard the 2-4

Your Crib: discard the 5-Jack
Jake's Crib: discard the 2-9

Pegging

Pegging! This is the fun part of Cribbage! This is where the action is! The bantering, the faking, the psychological warfare . . . the thinking part of Cribbage. Many a game is won or lost on a single bluff, a single misplay, a single gamble. About one-third of all points are scored by Pegging. Give this aspect of the game some serious study. Until you master the art of Pegging, your game will be mired in mediocrity. As Lord Kelvin would say, "Your knowledge will be of a meager and unsatisfactory kind."

The nondealer *always* begins Pegging by playing the *first* card. The dealer *always* pegs at least one point. The nondealer *may* be held scoreless. These are the absolutes. From this basis, the sky's the limit. The peg may consist of only a single point being scored (by the dealer) up to the possibilities of scoring double pairs royal twice (four of a kind twice). You and your opponent both hold 7-7-5-5, for example. The 7's played first (seven, fourteen, twenty-one, twenty-eight . . . "Go"), then the 5's (five, ten, fifteen, twenty. . .one for last card) could send the total Pegging score skyrocketing to forty-four points!

Strategy becomes very important when Pegging. Your board position in relation to your opponent is carefully weighed. Do you play offense ("play on") or do you play defense ("play off")? Are you far behind and must gamble to catch up? Is your opponent threatening to peg out and win the game? Do you desperately need a few pegs to win? These questions must be answered *before* the first card is played. A more detailed analysis of Pegging is made later in the book, but for now, let's begin with basic strategy.

You are the nondealer, and the game is fairly even. You want to maintain or achieve a superior position by pegging *more* than your opponent. This will be difficult. The dealer has the advantage in Pegging, averaging about one Pegging point more per deal. Before you make that first play, think ahead . . . if Uncle Jake pairs your first card (or 15's your card), how will you retaliate? Try not to let Jake get two free points. Have a card that will counter his two-point play. For example, you have a 4-5-6-7. Lead the 4, and if Jake pairs it, making the count "Eight," counter with the 7 for "fifteen" and recoup your two points.

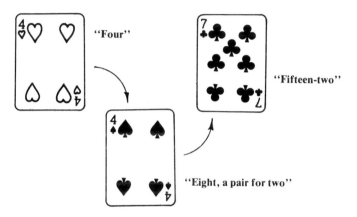

"Four" "Fifteen-two" "Eight, a pair for two"

The safest opening card is a card *below* the 5 (Ace-2-3-4), because your opponent cannot make a "fifteen" for two points. And his odds of scoring are at least 57% less than if you lead a 5 (heaven forbid!)or higher card. For example, you lead from a single 4: the deck contains only three more 4's that can score . . . or three chances. If you lead from a single 9: the deck contains three more 9's *plus* four 6's that can score . . . seven chances. Or 57% more risk! And the 5 lead? Sixteen 10-cards plus three 5's . . . nineteen chances to score! This would be a mistake, to say the least. If you lead from a pair of 4's, or from three 4's, your lead is that much safer.

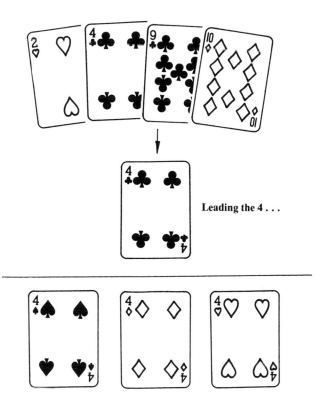

Leading the 4 . . .

. . . three chances to score

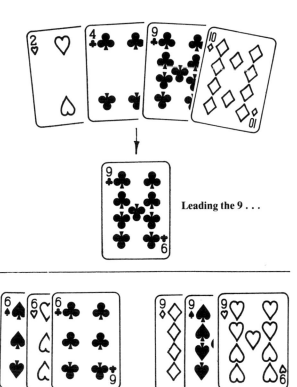

Leading the 9 . . .

. . . seven chances to score

Train yourself to think in this manner. Count the cards that can beat you—the "losers"—and play the odds. *Don't play hunches!* Players who play hunches, or guess and ignore the odds, are losers. When in doubt, figure the odds. How many cards are out that will beat me this way . . . and how many cards will beat me that way? Don't forget your discard to the Crib. And by all means consider the Starter card. There will be days on end that the long odds prevail, but hang in there. The law of averages *is* alive and well.

At times you will want to trade points ("play on") even if you come out on the short end of the score. This occurs primarily near the end of the game when a few extra points will allow you to peg out, or peg close enough to allow your hand (if you have first count) to score the 121st point and game. For example, you hold 3-5-6-7. "Playing on," you lead the 7, hoping to entice Jake to play an 8 for a "fifteen." If successful, you play your 6 for "twenty-one" and a desperately needed three points. Jake may score an easy run of four with a 9 play, but the sacrifice is worth the much needed three points. When jockeying for position earlier in the game, the 3-card would be the safer lead from the 3-5-6-7 hand.

If you are the dealer, you will have the advantage of seeing the first card before making a play. Once again, think before you play. Jake, the nondealer, leads a King, for example. Assume he has 10- and 5-cards since the King logically combines with other 10-cards to form runs, and with the 5-card to form 15's. If you are holding a 3-6-7-8, play the 8. If Jake plays the logical 10-card, you have the 3 for a "thirty-one" and two points. Playing the 3 on Jake's King lead would be a bad play, since it would allow Jake to "fifteen" the play with any 2's he may be holding. Remember . . . count the losers.

A common dilemma confronting the dealer is whether to pair the nondealer's first lead. According to one Cribbage expert, if a player pairs the lead, he will average .7 points on the plus side of the ledger. But other factors must be considered. If a player *always* pairs a lead, if possible, then his opponent will *always* lead from a pair, if possible. This cuts the .7 average profit down somewhat.

Nevertheless, it *is* profitable to pair a lead, as a general rule. But look at the board position. Can you risk a six-point peg? Do you *really* need the two points? Are you playing defense or offense? Do you have a safe defensive card, or are you trapped in a no-win

situation? For example, Uncle Jake leads a 2. You hold a 2-3-4-4. You are playing defense. Your first impulse might be to play a 4, but pairing the lead and risking the pairs royal (three of a kind) is the safest play. Remember, count the "losers." By pairing the 2 lead, leaves *two* losers (two Deuces remain in the deck). But by playing a 4 leaves *nine* losers (two 4's, three 3's, and four 9's). In this case, two losers vs. nine losers makes playing the 4 a very poor choice. Of course, some decisions are based upon your opponent's habits. You must know your board position. But, when in doubt, pair away!

The second card played by your opponent is the least risky to pair of the first three played. Of course, pairing the fourth card played is no risk at all. The reason pairing the third card is riskier than the second is because many players try to trap your last card with a pair for a seven-point play, or simply keep a pair for last in the event the opponent is forced to play out his remaining cards after getting a "Go." So, as a rule of thumb, *always* pair the second card *unless* a six-point peg will surely beat you! But keep a wary eye on Uncle Jake, who may get wise to your *consistent* style of play.

Study the diagrams for tips in Pegging. With a little practice, you will get the feel for the numbers. You will soon learn to "dump the lone Jack" (after the count is at twelve or above), not fall for the "sucker" plays, and play the odds.

Pegging Tips:

Lead the 7. If Jake pairs it, the Ace will add to "Fifteen." If Jake plays an 8 for "Fifteen," your 9 will form a run of three (and if Jake has the 6 for a run of four and "thirty," your Ace will recoup with a "thirty-one."

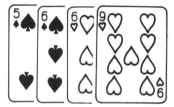

Lead the 6. If Jake pairs the 6 or plays a 9 for "Fifteen," you have covered your play.

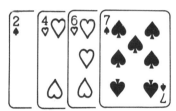

Lead the 4. If Jake pairs it, your 7 for "Fifteen" recovers your two points. In addition, the 4 lead's response is often a 9. Your 2 will make "Fifteen."

Lead the King. The least likely "Ten" card held by Jake will be a King. You do not want to entice a pair here.

Again, lead the King. It is the least likely "Ten" card held, and if Jake holds a 10, there is an excellent chance this will be his response, allowing you to pair it. The Queen or Jack lead would eliminate this chance.

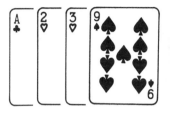

Lead the 3. If Jake pairs the lead, your 9 will counter for "Fifteen."

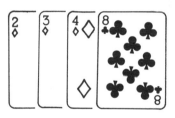

Lead the 3. This lead covers any "Ten" card response, and forces Jake's 5 or 6's off the play. Leading the 2 covers any "Ten" card responses also, but the 5 or 6 may respond instead of any "Ten" cards that you are fishing for.

Lead the 4. It will draw Jake's 9. Your 2 will then make "Fifteen." A King or Queen response by Jake can also be safely paired by you.

Jake leads a King

Play the 8 for "Eighteen." If Jake's logical second play is a "Ten" card for "Twenty-eight," your 3 scores "Thirty-one."

Jake leads a 2

Play the 5 for "Seven." You then have a chance to pair any Jack, Queen, or King that Jake may follow. The 5 would not allow Jake to play a 3 or 4 safely and would force any "Ten" cards into the open.

Jake leads an 8

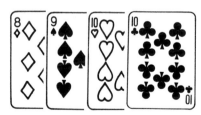

Pair the 8. You're trapped and the pair is the percentage play. Only two 8's are outstanding. If you play a 10, three 9's and two 10's can beat you (five cards vs. two cards. . .play the odds).

Now that you have learned the rules, know the basics of recognizing good hands, know the basics of discarding to the Crib, and have learned a bit about Pegging, well, Uncle Jake's winnings have suddenly shrunk dramatically. Now the best he can do is win about sixty-two out of 100. Now you can wager 2 to 1, even after having lost the cut for deal. But you still have a long way to go.

The game of Cribbage, basically simple, has many nuances. . .nuances that can gain a point or lose a point. And for every point you can add to your side of the ledger means about a 3% gain in victories. If you can average just *two points* more than Uncle Jake in a 121-point game, you should win fifty-three out of 100 games (a 6% edge). And that is the goal of this book. . .to make you the winner of fifty-three games against the expert! Sounds insignificant? Remember, this is Uncle Jake! Against lesser players, your average will be much higher!

Improving Your Game

ANALYZING YOUR GAME
DISCARDING TIPS
THE MAGIC ELEVEN
THE PEGGING TRAPS
TRAPPING THE FIVE
TRAPPING THE JACK
OTHER TRAPS
SLEEPER CARDS
ENTICING THE PLAY
PLAYING THE FLUSH
CRIBBAGE LOGIC
THE PERCENTAGE PLAY
END GAME PEGGING
CRIBBAGE PSYCHOLOGY
TURKEY PLAYS

Improving Your Game

Let's go through the game once again, picking up every possible point, every possible slip by your opponent, every possible advantage!

Let's begin with the cut for the deal. You are playing an average player and you feel your Cribbage skill is as good or better than his. Neither one of you has an aversion to wagering on the game. You win the first deal, then promptly say, "Hey, how about upping that wager? I feel lucky today." Actually, winning the cut gives you a 12% advantage! The first dealer will win fifty-six of 100 games, *on the average* (with equal skill levels, of course). There will be days on end when even the dealer can't win, but this wager will pay off as surely as the law of averages exists.

Now that you have won the deal, thoroughly shuffle the cards, making sure your opponent cannot see any of the cards, especially the bottom one. Having a knowledge of where any "extra" cards are—even one—can cost two points. . .or gain two points. When your opponent deals, keep your eyes on the deck. Careless shuffling by your opponent lets you see the Queen of spades on the bottom of the deck, for example. Your hand, after discarding, leaves you with the 10, Jack, Queen, and King. Naturally, you lead the "safe" card—the Queen. Train yourself to remember any and all cards seen. A cardinal sin would be to forget what you discarded to the Crib.

Since you won the deal, your opponent cuts for the Starter card. If he is careless, he may show you *another* card when he cuts the deck (and if he's a sharpie. . .he may sneak a pcek at the bottom card of the cut deck he holds). Sneaking a peek at the bottom card of the cut deck is unethical (in fact, it's down-

Careless card handling.

right cheating), but in the heat of a rapid-paced game, it's extremely easy to "sneak a peek." Insist that the top portion of the cut deck be held low and parallel to the playing surface. If your opponent persists in "sneaking a peek," call the hand a misdeal. This advantage, however slight, could mean the difference between winning and losing a close game.

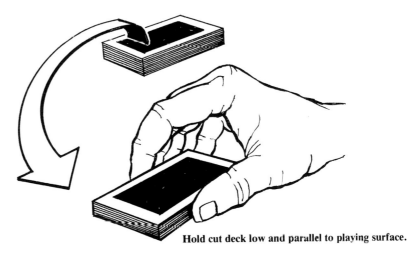

Hold cut deck low and parallel to playing surface.

Another sly point: watch your opponent shuffle the cards. Anything less than a thorough shuffle could give you the needed edge when playing the hand. By remembering what was played the preceding hand, could swing a decision in the right direction. For example, three 7's were played in the preceding hand. Your opponent leads a 7. . .do you pair the 7 or play your King? If you don't desperately need the two points, it may be wise to "lay off."

If you feel you are a more experienced player, by all means play at the fastest pace possible and yet keep your game under control. This rapid play will cause your opponent to try to maintain the pace, even though his game will suffer. His ego is at stake. Most players will try to keep up, even at the expense of their game. Conversely, if you are playing a better player, ignore his attempts at fast play. Keep your game *under control*. Play at your own pace. Think out your plays at your speed. Analyze the game thoroughly.

Discarding Tips

Discarding to your Crib, and to your opponent's Crib is one of the key aspects of the game. Don't rush this decision. Thoroughly think out your play. If it's your Crib, ask yourself these questions: Am I playing for maximum count? Am I defending Uncle Jake (he's near game and will probably need Pegging points)? Will the cards I'm keeping be good Pegging cards (cards the will shut out Uncle Jake's Pegging attempts)? If it's Jake's Crib, ask yourself: Do I need maximum count? Will the discards aid a potential high-scoring-hand? Are they good defensive cards? Does your discard cut the odds of a good Crib? Do I need to be concerned with Uncle Jake's Crib? Think! Study the "Discarding Tips" diagrams. These tips will add to your discarding ability and give you some insights as to the type of thinking that should accompany discarding.

As you continue playing, this skill will improve. The adage, "Practice Make Perfect" is just as true in Cribbage as in any endeavor requiring skill. Many of the tips illustrated will demand modification when your skill level increases to the "expert" class.

Situation: second hand, Jake is black standing at fifteen. You are white standing at eleven. It is your Crib.

Q: Am I playing offense or defense?

A: Offense. It's your Crib, the game has just begun, and neither player has established a superior position.

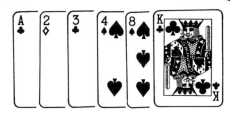

Discard the Ace-King. Many players make the mistake of keeping the run of four (Ace-2-3-4), discarding the 8-King. The 8-King discard weakens the Crib's chances of scoring—either the 8 or King is lost. With the Ace-King discard, *all* cards have an excellent chance of scoring. If a 2-3-4 is cut for Starter, the hand counts twelve (maximum) . . .and only ten if the Ace-2-3-4 hand is held.

Discard the 5-10. The chances of Jake discarding "Ten" cards to your Crib are very good. And the 2 works with your basic 6-7-8. Once again, the run of four does *not* always score maximum, as a 6-7-8 Starter will score fourteen (as will a 5 Starter), but the 5-10 discard to your Crib is preferable to the 2-10 discard.

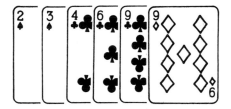

Discard the 6-9 of clubs. Since it's Jake's Pegging lead, the 2-3-4-9 hand is superior to the 2-3-4-6. The 2-9 is a better offensive-defensive combination against the "ten" card lead than is the 2-6 combination.

Discard the Queen-King. A 7-Queen or King discard weakens the Crib's chances of scoring. And if Jake leads a "ten" card? What an opportunity for a Pegging bonanza!

Discard the 7-8. Once again, any other discard would either weaken your hand or the Crib. Make all your cards count, if possible.

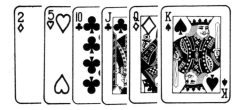

Discard the 2-King. The other alternative is the 2-10, but the King has the best chance of being discarded by Jake.

Discarding Tips

Situation: Jake is black standing at fifty-three. You are white standing at thirty-one. It is Jake's Crib.

Q: Am I playing offense or defense?

A: Desperation offense.

Q: Do I need being concerned about balking Jake's Crib?

A: Yes, but you must gamble to have any hope of winning the game. Play for maximum count.

Discard the 7-8. A 5-Queen Starter will score a maximum sixteen points (seventeen with Nobs). The odds are roughly 3-1 Jake will *not* match your 7-8 discard. Many beginning Cribbage players play too conservatively and destory a strong potential hand—especially in situations pictured above.

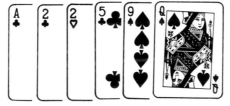

Discard the 5-9. If you are fortunate and cut a 3 Starter, you will score a maximum fourteen points (a 2 Starter will score twelve).

Go for broke. Discard the 7-Queen. The odds of cutting the 5 are 11½ to 1 but, if successful, you're back in the game.

Discard a pair of Aces. Then lead a 7. If Jake pairs your lead, the remaining Ace scores fifteen-two. If you are lucky, the 7 lead may entice Jake's 8 (for fifteen-two), and you respond with your 8 for a "gambling" twenty-three. With a break this may be a "Go" and you score pairs royal for thirty-one (and eight big pegs). And the Ace-7-8-8 hand, with a 6 Starter, will score a maximum sixteen points.

Discard the Jack-King. The Ace-Ace-5-9 will score twelve points with an Ace-5-9 Starter (maximum for this hand). And by holding the lone 5, you have slightly reduced Jake's Crib scoring chances.

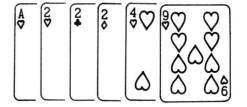

Discard the 4-9. The sixteen outstanding "ten" cards, if cut for the Starter, give you an easy twelve. A 3 Starter will score fifteen points. Ignore the heart flush.

44

Discarding Tips

Situation: Jake is black standing at 115, needing six points to win the game. You are white standing at 114 points. It is your Crib.

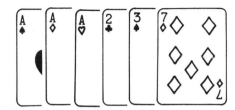

Discard the 2-3. If Jake's hand consists of "ten" cards-5's, you have an excellent chance to peg seven points to win the game. This is an ideal Pegging hand.

Q: What are Jake's chances of scoring six points?

A: Jake will score *at least six* points about 88% of the time when he is the nondealer (study the charts in chapter five "What's the Odds?")

Q: Is it possible to peg seven points and win the game?

A: Analyze the cards dealt to you and decide.

Q: If my cards do *not* give me a chance to peg seven points, how do I play the hand?

A: Discard your hand to play *maximum* defense. Then play for that meager 12% chance you have to hold Jake to less than six points.

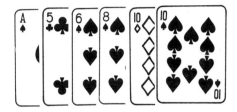

Discard the 10-10. Your best hope of winning the game: Jake must lead a 7 and you respond with your 8 for fifteen-two, then Jake plays his 9 for twenty-four (a run of three). You respond with your 6 for thirty (a run of four), and with luck, a "Go" to win the game. Other Pegging chances exist but your odds of scoring seven points are severely limited, if Jakes does *not* lead a 7.

Discard the 3-Jack. Your chances of pegging seven are slim. Play defense and hope for the best. Do *not* play your 5 on a "ten" lead. Play your 6.

Discard the 10-King of spades. Keep your Jacks for last in a desperation Jack trap for seven points. And keep the King of diamonds for a possible flush fake.

Discard the 10-Jack. Your chances of Pegging seven are practically zero. Play defense and hope for the best. The King is a better defensive card than the 10 or Jack.

The Magic Eleven!

Cards that total eleven are especially important in Pegging. The 5-6, 7-4, 8-3, 9-2, and "ten-card"-Ace combinations aid offensively and defensively in Pegging. These eleven combinations are especially important when you need a strong defense. When Jake needs a couple of peg points to win the game, make every effort to keep a "Magic Eleven." The reasons are obvious. Sixteen "ten" cards (combined with 5's) are one of the most common hands held. And since 5's are rarely led in Pegging, the "ten" cards are played first. The "Magic Eleven" easily scores thirty-one. . .shutting out Jake, and scoring for you. If you are playing desperation defense and don't have two cards totaling eleven, try to keep three cards that total eleven. For example, 5-3-3, 9-Ace-Ace, 8-2-Ace, 7-2-2, 6-3-2. It's amazing how often this "eleven" defense works.

Even if defense is not of prime importance, when studying your six cards and an obvious discard is tough to figure, base your decision on the "Magic Eleven." Keep cards that total eleven. Your score in Pegging will improve.

The basic combinations of the "Magic Eleven."

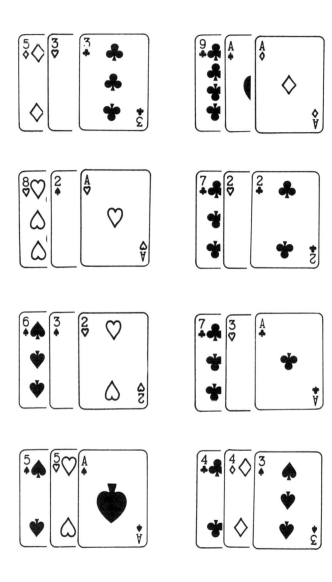

Three-card combinations of the "Magic Eleven."

And your defense will improve! An example of a tough hand to discard: Ace-2-6-9-Jack-King. Discard the Jack and King instead of the 6-9. Even though the Jack and King, combined with the Ace, adds to eleven, the 9-2 combination is preferable. Since the "Magic Eleven" is especialy designed to stop "ten" card leads, your Jack and King, combined with the Ace, are not nearly as effective as the 9-2. If Jake plays a 10 or Jack first, play your 2. But if Jake plays a Queen or King first, play your 9.

This is obvious if you think it out. A 9 played on a Jack or 10 lead gives Jake the opportunity to score a three-card run. Playing the 2 on his lead gives Jake a chance for a "fifteen-two" play, but this is the least risky of the two alternatives. However, play your 9 on the Queen or King lead as there is no risk of a three-card run.

Another example: Ace-2-6-Jack-Queen-King (opponent's Crib). Discard the 2-6, keeping the "eleven" combinations intact. And the odds for hitting the Starter card for maximum remain the same, whether you hold the Ace or 2 with the Jack-Queen-King. Holding the Ace, eight cards will give you a nine-point hand (4-4-4-4-5-5-5-5). Holding the 2, again eight cards will give you a nine-point hand (3-3-3-3-5-5-5-5). Holding the Ace will give you that little extra edge in Pegging.

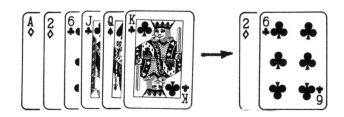

Examples of Playing the "Magic Eleven"

Your Crib: discard the 2-King (defense); the 2-6 (offense).
Jake's Crib: discard the 2-King.
When playing defense the 5-6 ("eleven") is the key, especially when it's your Crib, and defensing Jake's possible "ten" card lead.

Your Crib: discard the 10-King.
Jake's Crib: again discard the 10-King.
The 4-7 ("eleven") will improve your Pegging score. Your lead? Play the 4 and cover your play.

Your Crib: Discard the Queen-King.
Jake's Crib: Discard the 10-King.
The 3-3-5 will pay off two ways: a 4 cut will give you a twelve hand, the 3-3-5 is another "Magic Eleven."

Your Crib: discard the 10-Queen.
Jake's Crib: discard the 8-Queen. Lead the 3.
The "Magic Eleven" isn't quite as effective when you're the nondealer and leading the first card (in this case defensing Jake's Crib is more important than keeping the 3-8).

Your Crib: discard the Ace-Queen (defense); the Ace-2 (offense).
Jake's Crib: discard the Ace-Queen. Lead the 2. If Jake is holding four "ten" cards, the 2-9 "eleven" will work for you. And the 2 is a much better Pegging lead than the 9 (your logical lead if you held the 9-10-Jack-Queen).

Your Crib: discard the Jack-King.
Jake's Crib: discard the 8-King. Lead the 9.
You have an excellent chance to peg four points with your Aces ("thirty-thirty-one") if Jake holds a Queen or King.
The Ace-Ace-9 covers the "eleven."

Your Crib: discard the Queen-King.
Jake's Crib: discard the 7-King.
The 2-2-7 covers the "Magic Eleven." And defense dictates the 7-King discard to Jake's Crib.

Your Crib: discard the Jack-King.
Jake's Crib: discard the 9-King (defense), the 7-9 (offense).
Holding the 2-2-7-9 gives you two "Magic Eleven's" (7-2-2 and 2-9).

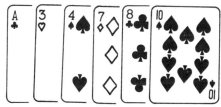

Your Crib: discard the Ace-10 (defense); the 7-8 (offense).
Jake's Crib: discard the Ace-10.
The double "eleven's" (3-8, 4-7) will improve your Pegging count.

The Pegging Traps

Setting traps in Pegging can net tidy sums of points and can be the deciding factor in the game. The *easiest* card to trap is the 5, the next easiest to trap is the Jack, then the Ace, the 2, and then the 3.

The Nondealer 5-card Trap

First, let's trap the 5. The most common hand in Cribbage is "ten" cards combined with one or more 5's. In fact, this hand will be played about one time in four. This hand offers several varieties of traps. Let's describe the hands you must hold if you're the nondealer and playing the first Pegging card. The slickest and easiest trap: your hand must contain three key cards, 6-6-4. Lead a 6. Jake cannot play his 5 (this would allow you to score an easy three-card run) and is forced to play a "ten" card. You play another 6. . . and the trap is sprung! Jake must play a 5, making the count twenty-seven. You follow with your 4 for thirty-one. . .a run of three and two points for thirty-one. A total of five points. Poor Jake comes up empty! This play works whether Jake has one or two 5's.

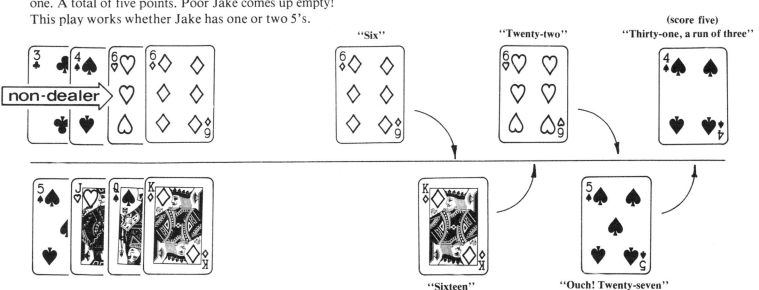

Another variation of the 5 trap: Uncle Jake must have two 5's to spring the trap so it is a little tougher to pull off. In this case, you must have four key cards: 6-7-7-"ten" (the second 7 could also be an 8 or 9). Lead the second 7 (or the 8 or 9), and almost certainly, Jake will respond with a safe "ten" card. You respond with your "sleeper ten" (if you're lucky, you'll get a pair for two points). If the trap works, this will be a "Go." Jake is forced to lead his remaining "ten" card. You respond with your 7, forcing the trapped 5's into the open to run the count to twenty-two. You then add your 6 for a run of three and a "Go" for four.

Both traps usually net five points for you, and one point for Uncle Jake. A profit of four points Pegging when you're the nondealer is excellent.

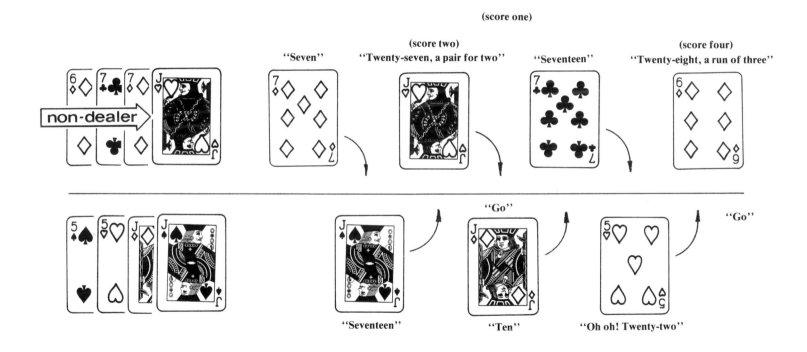

The Dealer 5-card Trap

Trapping the 5 when you're the dealer: the key is at least two cards that combine with a 5 to form a run (3-4, 4-6, 6-7) and then Pegging so that Uncle Jake cannot safely "dump" his 5 (or 5's) without risking retaliation of a pair or run. Let's go through one example of the dealer trapping a 5: You are the dealer and hold 3-6-7-8. Jake leads a King. Respond with your 8 for eighteen. Jake may "dump" his 5 here, but the odds are he will play a "ten" card trying for the "Go" at the count of twenty-eight. However, you play your 3 for thirty-one. The trap is sprung. Jake is forced to lead his remaining "ten" card (leading the 5 is unthinkable), followed by your 7 for seventeen. Jake's trapped 5 is played (twenty-two) and you follow with your 6 for a run of three and a "Go"—scoring four points. This trap nets five or six points, and results in Jake being blanked.

The trap has a good chance of suceeding if Jake has two 5's. But the odds are he will dump a 5 at the count of eighteen, and escape the trap. A player of lesser skill probably would *not* dump his 5 at this point, and would be trapped. The key to the trap is, of course, keeping the 3-4, 4-6, or in the example, the 6-7, for your last two cards to catch your opponent's 5.

This example also illustrates the advantage of keeping a "Magic Eleven." For example, your hand contains a 3-6-7-8-9-King. You are both within Pegging range to win the game. Discard the 9-King (ordinarily a poor discard to *your* Crib). The chance of a 5 trap, plus a Pegging shutout (and keeping a "Magic Eleven") make this the correct play.

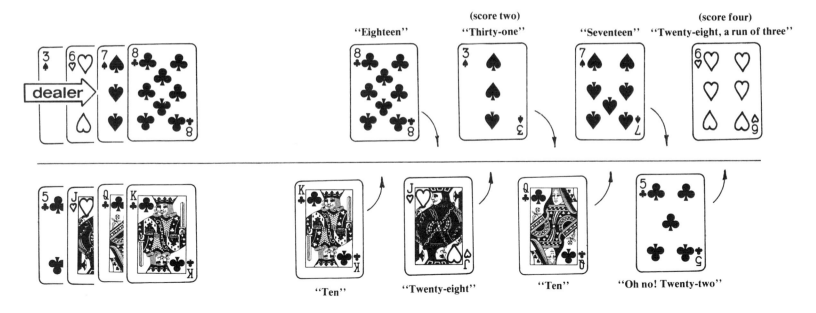

Trapping the Jack

The second easiest card to trap is the Jack. Regardless of who is the dealer, save a pair of Jacks for last, and it will amaze you how often the trap works. If you have a Jack-Jack-Queen-King, for example, lead the King. Most players will respond with the safer 5-card here, rather than pair the King risking a six-peg. If you lead one of your Jacks, and Jake holds a 5-Jack, the 5 is usually played, and the opportunity for trapping the Jack is lost. The "ten" card lead will usually draw a 5 response. Keep your Jacks for your last two cards to spring this trap.

On the other hand, if you have a *single* Jack, "dump" it at the first safe opportunity (with the count twelve or higher). *The lone Jack is a liability.* This is one of the most common errors that beginning, or even average, players make. Remember, "dump" the lone Jack when the count is at least "twelve," making a retaliatory pairing impossible.

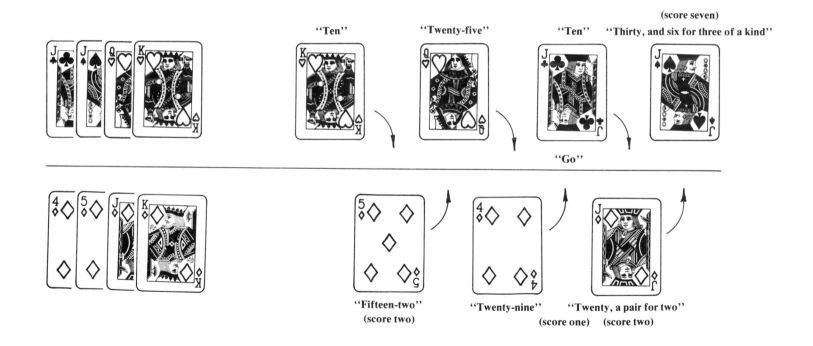

Other Traps

Another excellent trap play occurs when Uncle Jake leads an 8 or 7, while you are holding the combination of 4-5-6. Entice a run with your 6. If Jake has led an 8, your 6 for "Fourteen" may entice his 7 for "twenty-one." Jake may be trapped! Add your 5 to the run for "twenty-six." A good chance exists that this will be a "Go," and you add your 4 for a run of five! And a "Go"! This combination results in Jake pegging three and with you pegging ten! A tidy profit, indeed! This is an especially good play if you're holding a 4-5-6-6. If Jake decides to pair your first 6, you counter with pairs-royal. A no-lose situation. But don't employ this trap when playing defensively, as even a profit of seven points is worthless if it allows Jake to peg into range to win game. Conversely, if you lead an 8 or 7, and Jake plays a 6, take a very wary look at your hand. Do you have a 5 or 4 to cut off this "sucker" play? If you don't, think twice before creating the run of three.

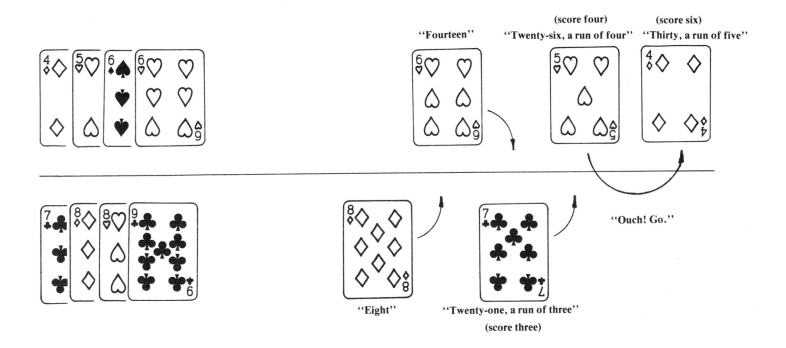

"Fourteen"
(score four) "Twenty-six, a run of four"
(score six) "Thirty, a run of five"

"Ouch! Go."

"Eight" "Twenty-one, a run of three"

(score three)

53

Trapping low value cards—with the Ace being the easiest to trap—is simply accomplished by running the count to "twenty-nine" (if you're holding two Aces) with one of the Aces, hoping Uncle Jake has a lone Ace for "thirty," then adding your last Ace for "thirty-one" and a tidy eight points. With a pair of Deuces, you run the count to "twenty-seven" with the first Deuce. With 3's, run the count to "twenty-five" with the first 3. In all cases, the trap, if it works, nets a profit of six points. Five points if "thirty-one" is not reached exactly. A variation is to run the count to "thirty" with the first of your two Aces, hoping to pair yourself for a "free" four points. Running the count to "twenty-nine" with the first of your two Deuces, and to "twenty-eight" with the first of your two 3's has the same result. But this play runs the risk of backfiring! Uncle Jake may have the third Ace, 2, or 3 and nail you. Board position becomes the dominant factor in running a risk of this nature.

The key to setting pegging traps is *thinking ahead*! After taking a look at Uncle Jake's first card, and the Starter card, quickly make the best estimate possible of the logical hand that Jake is holding. Consider your hand, also, when making this estimate. After seeing Jake's second card, rethink your estimate. After seeing two cards, your estimating becomes much easier, and, of course, the third card will help that much more in predicting the fourth card. After making your best estimate of Jake's hand, set your traps! Keep thinking!

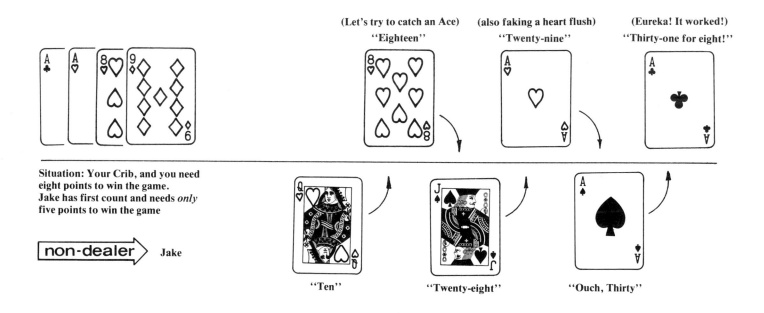

Situation: Your Crib, and you need eight points to win the game. Jake has first count and needs *only* five points to win the game

non-dealer > Jake

(Let's try to catch an Ace)
"Eighteen"

(also faking a heart flush)
"Twenty-nine"

(Eureka! It worked!)
"Thirty-one for eight!"

"Ten"   "Twenty-eight"   "Ouch, Thirty"

"Sleeper" Cards

For every offense, there's a defense. Knowing that Jake will be analyzing *your hand* after taking a look at your first card, lead your "sleeper" card. A sleeper is a card that is a mismatch in a good Cribbage hand. For example, in a 7-Jack-Queen-King hand, the 7 is a "sleeper." Lead the 7. Camouflage your hand as long as possible. Make Uncle Jake guess which side of a sequence your third or fourth card falls on. For example, you are holding a 10-10-Jack-Queen. Don't play the 10, then the Queen, as the void between the 10 and Queen makes the Jack in your hand obvious. Play the Jack. Uncle Jake may wrongly surmise you are holding a 9. Conversely, if you are holding a poor hand, by purposely leaving a void, Jake may wrongly surmise you're holding the card in the void. This deception makes your odds a little better of scoring on Jake's subsequent plays.

If you're playing offense (playing on) and want to pair as much as possible, lead from the *end* of a sequence of four cards. For example, the 9-10-Jack-Queen should begin with the 9 lead. A good possibility exists of a Queen pair with the 9 lead, but quickly diminishes with the 10 lead, and practically disappears with the Jack lead. In addition, this play cuts down on the possibility of Jake scoring the "thirty-one" followup if he happens to have a 6 for "fifteen-two." You follow with the "dumped" Jack for "twenty-five." Since a 6 has already been played, the *odds* are lessened for Jake to follow with another 6 for "thirty-one." In this case, Jake may be forced to play a 5 for "thirty" and a "Go." This makes your following 10 lead that much safer. In this case, "dumping" the Jack with your second card creates a 9-void-Jack, but the lone Jack is more of a liability than exposing a probable 10.

"sleeper"   "sleeper"   "sleeper"

Enticing the Play

Beware of the enticed play. If you lead a 4, for example, and Jake plays an 8, the odds are good he has a 3-card, enticing you to play a 3 for "fifteen." He then counters with *his* 3 for a pair, recouping the two points. Or he has backed his play with another 8. A good player will always attempt to play a card with another card backing his play. For example, Jake plays to "sixteen" and your remaining cards are a 3-6-7. Play the 6 for "twenty-two." If Jake pairs the 6 for "twenty-eight," the play is covered by the 3 for "thirty-one." Playing the 3 or 7 on the "sixteen" would be "free" for Jake to pounce on. This style of play is critical to good Cribbage. Think ahead! Try to get at least a trade when Pegging. Give Uncle Jake nothing for free.

Of course, there will be times when your hand is in a hopeless bind and even Houdini couldn't save the day. Take your lumps and come back strong on the next hand. Be an optimist. A positive attitude (and playing the odds) is conducive to winning. A pessimistic attitude will put you in the loser's column. Study the examples of enticing the play. This skill is extremely important and must be mastered for you to become a winning player. . .a winning player against the "snake"!

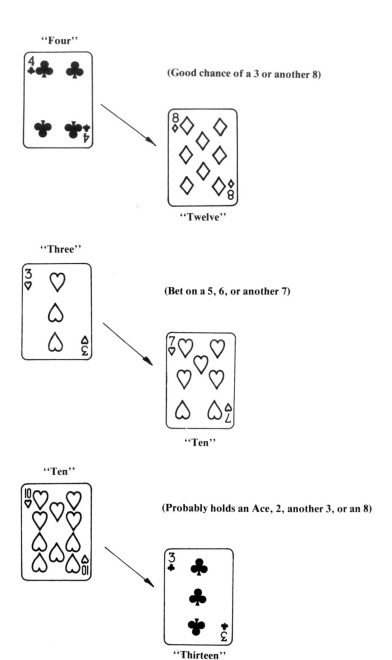

"Four"

(Good chance of a 3 or another 8)

"Twelve"

"Three"

(Bet on a 5, 6, or another 7)

"Ten"

"Ten"

(Probably holds an Ace, 2, another 3, or an 8)

"Thirteen"

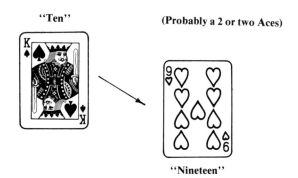

"Ten"

(Probably a 2 or two Aces)

"Nineteen"

56

Playing the Flush

A flush is held about once in every six hands. On many occasions when pegging, a tough decision may be made by either "faking a flush" or playing your opponent for a flush (after seeing one or more of his cards). When discarding to the Crib, whether yours or Uncle Jake's, keep the flush possibilities in mind. When you have the opportunity, place two cards of the same suit in *your* Crib, and balk Jake's Crib with cards of different suits. This is a very subtle point as you rarely cash in this play nor does this defense rarely pays off in Jake's Crib. But many times the discard can be made without affecting the count of the hand. Don't get careless and overlook the flush possibilities. Perhaps once in 100 games you'll collect five big points for a flush in the Crib, and once in 100 games you'll stop a five-point bonus in Jake's Crib by simply not getting careless.

And there will be times when you must break up a pair of Jacks and give Jake a Jack in his Crib. Study your hand. Which Jack is of the shorter suit? For example, you have a 4-5-6-8-Jack-Jack. You discard the 8 and a Jack to Jake's Crib. You have the Jack of Hearts and the Jack of Clubs. The Jack of Hearts is your only heart. The Jack of Clubs is matched by the 4 of Clubs. Give Jake the Jack of Clubs. The deck (and Jake's hand) contains twelve more hearts and only eleven more clubs. This gives you a 1/46th (about 2%) better chance to cut a heart for the Starter, giving *you* the point for nobs. How sweet it is when it pays off!

Another subtle tip when pegging: fake a flush as long as you can (without making obvious boo-boos, of course). For example, you hold a 4-4-5-6 with the 4 of Clubs, and the other 4-5-6 are hearts. Lead the 4 of Hearts. You will be able to fake a flush if

the opportunity arises. This play is wasted on most Cribbage players. But when you move in tougher circles, every edge is analyzed. A good player will "take" a flush fake from time to time. Train yourself to make this play. Again, don't let discarding two cards of the same suit influence Crib discarding selection, as the play is too subtle to pay off very often. Again, how sweet it is when it finally pays off!

Check the diagrams to see how flushes influence play:

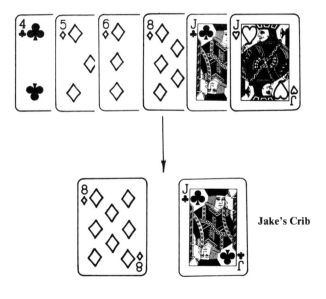

Jake's Crib

2% is 2%!

How Flushes Influence Play

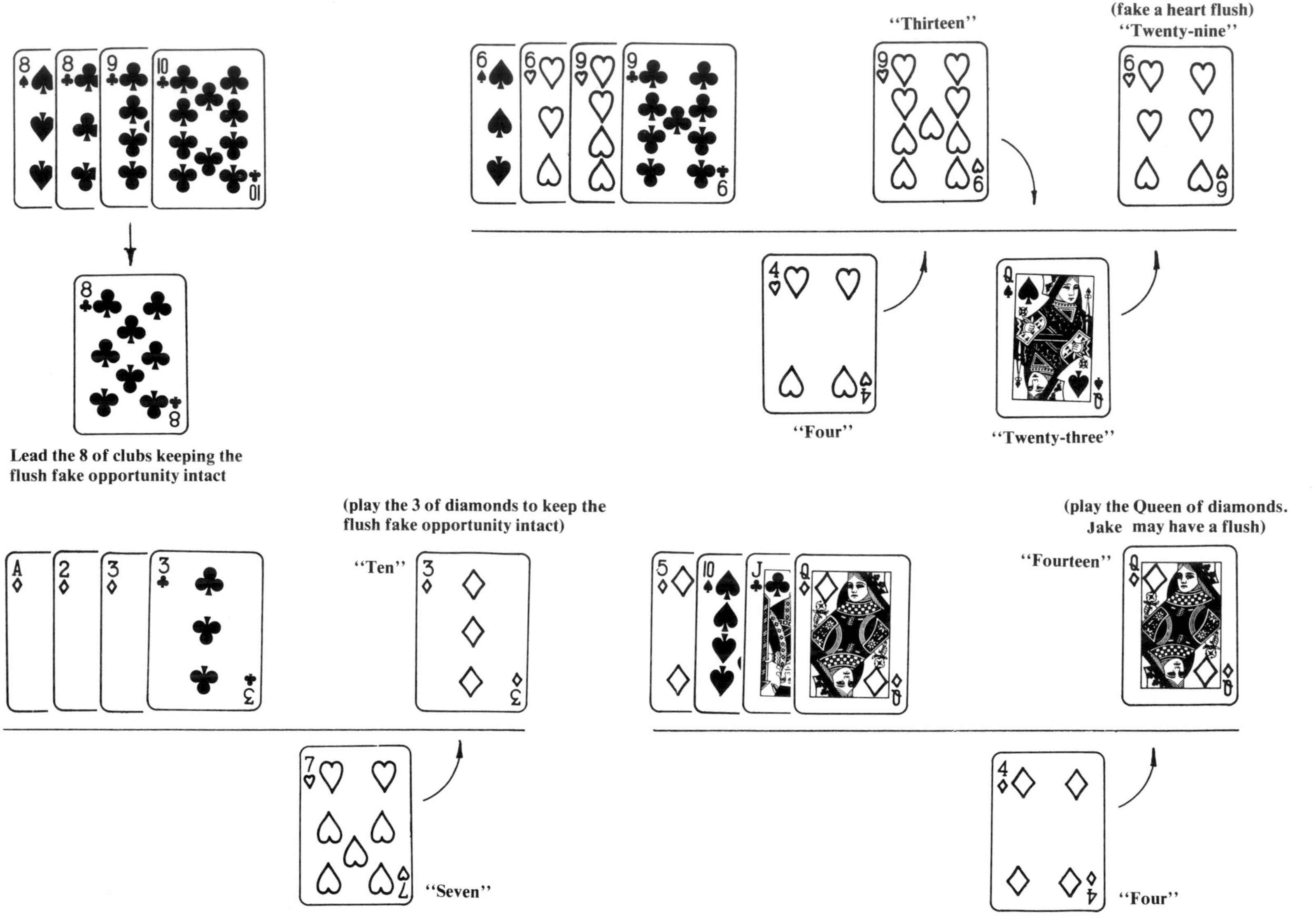

Lead the 8 of clubs keeping the
flush fake opportunity intact

"Thirteen"

(fake a heart flush)
"Twenty-nine"

"Four"

"Twenty-three"

(play the 3 of diamonds to keep the
flush fake opportunity intact)

"Ten"

"Seven"

(play the Queen of diamonds.
Jake may have a flush)

"Fourteen"

"Four"

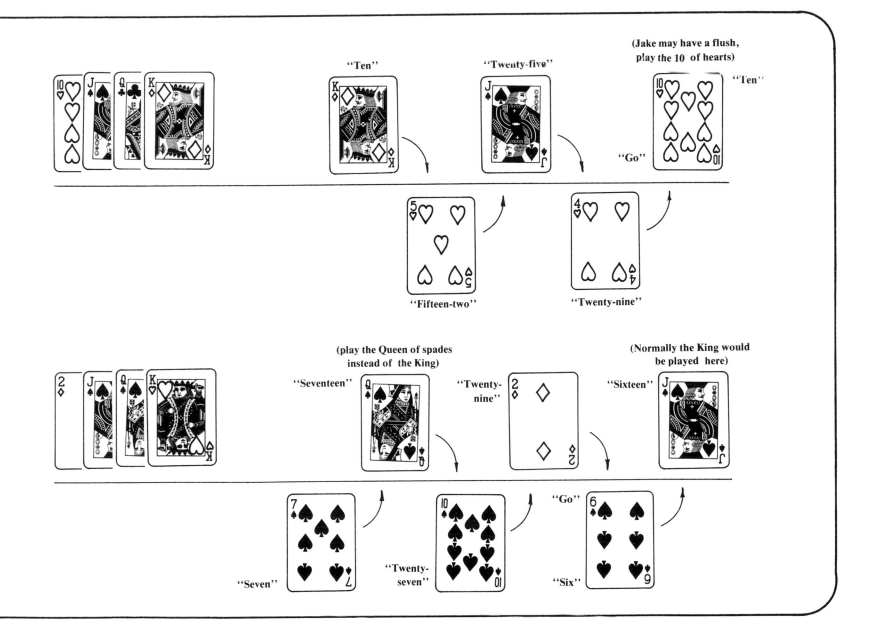

(Jake may have a flush, play the 10 of hearts)

"Ten"   "Twenty-five"   "Ten"

"Go"

"Fifteen-two"   "Twenty-nine"

(play the Queen of spades instead of the King)   **(Normally the King would be played here)**

"Seventeen"   "Twenty-nine"   "Sixteen"

"Seven"   "Twenty-seven"   "Go"   "Six"

59

a "ten"...
or an Ace

Logic

Logic! A five-letter word for *thinking*! After playing several hundred games of Cribbage, standard plays will become apparent. You will be able to develop "X-ray" vision, a la Superman, *if you work at it*! This is especially true when playing accomplished players like old Jake, the "snake." Beginning players make too many mistakes to allow the full play of logic, but, of course, it works to some degree on all players.

A winning Cribbage player must be able to "read" his opponent's hand rapidly. This ability is acquired through study, practice, and critical observation of your opponent's habits and style of play. Surprisingly, the better the player, the easier it is to apply logic to read his game. . .his cards.

Beginners play hunches, make unorthodox plays, and will surprise you with a poor play. These hunches and unorthodox plays, though confusing to the good player, will still lead to defeat for the beginner. And despite being able to "read" the good player's hand by applying logic, the good player will be tougher to defeat. The good player's game is based upon playing the odds, applying his analysis of your game, and his hard, cold logic. . .a very tough combination to beat. Without applying logic of your own, the consistent logical play from the good player will beat you. But by applying good, sound logic, you will, at worst, play to a stalemate, and at best, come out victorious.

Let's have an example of how to apply logic. Your analysis of Uncle Jake's board position indicates he will be playing defensively. As the nondealer he leads a Queen. Immediately, you may deduce he does *not* have the small five combinations (1-4, 2-3) or any 2's, 3's, or 4's, nor does he have a King (unless he has two or more Queens). Why? A defensive play would be a lead from any 2-3-4 (a 57% less chance of your opponent scoring on a small card lead—three losers vs. seven losers if a lone Queen is led). Jake may have a lone Ace, 5's, or he may have led a "sleeper" Queen to his basic hand of 6-7-8-9 combinations. But his lead has, by logic, almost certainly ruled out any 2-3-4 cards remaining in his hand.

You play a 5 on the Queen lead for "fifteen-two." Jake plays a Jack for "twenty-five." You now deduce Jake has all "ten" cards remaining, probably another Queen and a 10, with a lone Ace or King a possibility. Why? If he had two Jacks, he would not "dump" one here, but would "dump" a lone "ten" card (the most likely lone "ten" card to be "dumped" is the Jack). If Jake *does* have two Jacks,

60

then he also has two Queens (with the Queen being the first play. . .the safer defensive play). And since Jake did *not* pair your 5, his chances of having a 5 have dimmed (unless he's playing desperation defense, and pairs royal would surely beat him). After seeing Jake's first two cards, logic decrees that the remaining two cards are, in order of probability, Queen, 10, King, Jack, and Ace. Since the Queen play was followed by a Jack, the Queen was not a "sleeper," but part of a basic "ten" card combination.

You play a 6 for "thirty-one." Jake begins a new sequence with another Queen. Now logic tells you the odds are that the remaining card is most likely a 10 or a King, the next most likely card would be a Jack, then an Ace. . .and then any "sleeper" cards (6-7-8-9)

or a third Queen. You would then play a card that Jake would *not* logically have in his hand—a 2, 3, or 4. You hold a 3 and a 4. You play the 3 for "thirteen" (remember, logic decrees Jake may have an Ace—if you played the 4 for "fourteen," Jake could play an Ace for "fifteen-two").

Jake does have an Ace for "fourteen." You complete play with your 4 for "eighteen" and a "Go."

Applying logic has saved two points (not allowing Jake the last "fifteen-two") has not cost you, playing offensively, points.

Study the examples of applying logic. They are the ultimate key to playing winning Cribbage.

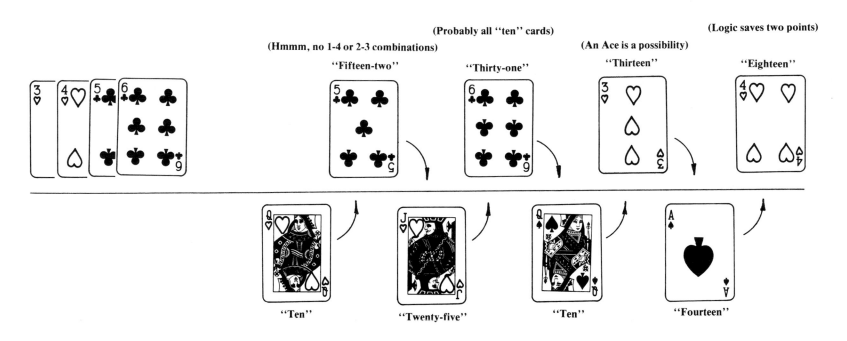

(Hmmm, no 1-4 or 2-3 combinations)
(Probably all "ten" cards)
(An Ace is a possibility)
(Logic saves two points)

"Fifteen-two" "Thirty-one" "Thirteen" "Eighteen"

"Ten" "Twenty-five" "Ten" "Fourteen"

Applying Logic

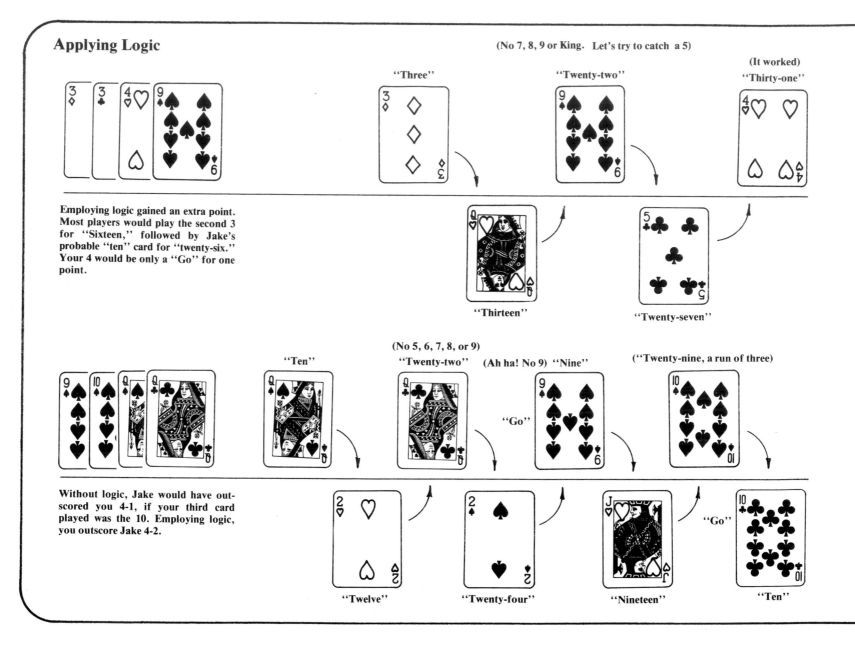

(No 7, 8, 9 or King. Let's try to catch a 5)

"Three"   "Twenty-two"   **(It worked)** "Thirty-one"

Employing logic gained an extra point. Most players would play the second 3 for "Sixteen," followed by Jake's probable "ten" card for "twenty-six." Your 4 would be only a "Go" for one point.

"Thirteen"   "Twenty-seven"

(No 5, 6, 7, 8, or 9)

"Ten"   "Twenty-two"   (Ah ha! No 9) "Nine"   ("Twenty-nine, a run of three)

"Go"

Without logic, Jake would have out-scored you 4-1, if your third card played was the 10. Employing logic, you outscore Jake 4-2.

"Twelve"   "Twenty-four"   "Nineteen"   "Go"   "Ten"

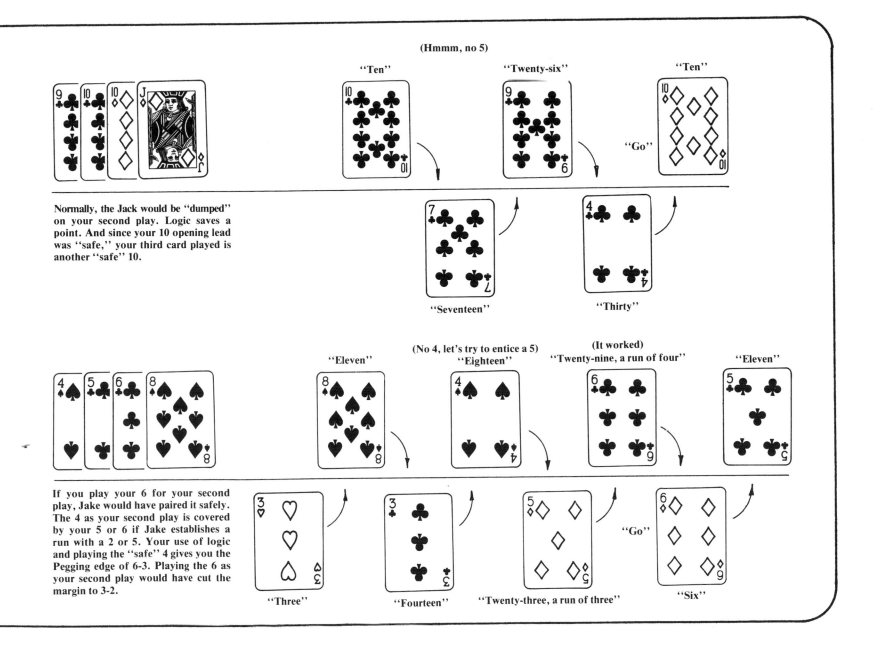

(Hmmm, no 5)

"Ten" "Twenty-six" "Ten"

"Go"

"Seventeen" "Thirty"

Normally, the Jack would be "dumped" on your second play. Logic saves a point. And since your 10 opening lead was "safe," your third card played is another "safe" 10.

(No 4, let's try to entice a 5) (It worked)
"Eleven" "Eighteen" "Twenty-nine, a run of four" "Eleven"

"Go"

"Three" "Fourteen" "Twenty-three, a run of three" "Six"

If you play your 6 for your second play, Jake would have paired it safely. The 4 as your second play is covered by your 5 or 6 if Jake establishes a run with a 2 or 5. Your use of logic and playing the "safe" 4 gives you the Pegging edge of 6-3. Playing the 6 as your second play would have cut the margin to 3-2.

The Percentage Play

Cribbage is a numbers game, and certain numbers combine with other numbers in a logical manner to form the runs, the fifteen's, and the pairs. These logical combinations can be played *offensively* and *defensively* to your best advantage if you study the odds and make the *percentage* play.

It's surprising how many players—even experienced players—misplay these common combinations. In most cases, these players have fallen into the trap of habitual play, and have ceased to *think*. And without thinking, the percentage play slips away. Many times it slips away unnoticed. Other times the play is recognized too late and the "golden opportunity" is lost. And in many cases, this opportunity was simply missed because the *percentage play* was not recognized.

The following diagrams illustrate a few plays that are misplayed regularly by many players. Study the combinations, and play the percentage way, and your Pegging score will certainly improve, both offensively and defensively.

The Percentage Play

The Ace-4 (or Ace-4-4). . .lead the 4

Leading the 4 forces Jake's 5 or 6 off the play, increasing your odds of catching a "ten" card. Leading the Ace allows Jake to safely play a 5-6-8-9.

The 2-3 (or Ace-2-3, 2-3-4). . .lead the 3

The 3 lead forces Jake's 4-5-6 off the play. The 2 lead allows Jake to safely play a 5 or 6. You want to entice a "ten" card here.

The 6-7-8-"ten". . .lead the 8

The 8 lead keeps the 5-trap play intact. The King (or any "ten" card) would entice a 5 response (the very card you want to trap later).

The Ace-2-3-4. . .Jake's "ten" lead. . .play the 4

Middle card combinations vs. a "ten" lead

When Jake leads a "ten" card, odds dictate he holds all "ten" cards with a 5 or 5's. Playing a 4 on his "ten" lead forces the 5 off the play and keeps your Ace-2-3 run intact if Jake follows with another logical "ten" card for twenty-four. Play your 3 for twenty-seven for a likely "Go." Then collect your run of three.

The key to scoring with middle-value cards vs. a "ten" lead is to keep combinations that combine with Jake's probable 5 for a trap attempt.

Small combinations vs. a "ten" lead:

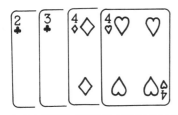 

The Ace-2-3-"ten". . .Jake's "ten" lead. . .play the Ace

The secret of scoring with the small-card combinations vs. the "ten" lead is holding your counters for last *and* running the count *over* twenty-six with your second play. In this example, if Jake plays a "ten" card for twenty-three, you counter with a 4 for twenty-seven, setting up your probable pair of 4's for thirty-one and four points.

If your hand is a 2-2-3-4, your first card played would be the 4, then the 3. If your hand is a 2-3-3-4, your first card played is again the 4, then the *3* (the 2 would be twenty-six. . . a no-no).

Playing a 2 or 3 on a "ten" lead instead of the Ace takes away your chances of scoring thirty-one if Jake has all "ten" cards. In playing desperation offense in this situation, play the Jack on the 10. Your play is covered by a thirty-one if Jake scores a run or pairs the Jack.

The Percentage Play: the Four-card Run

The 3-4-5-6 run is usually held as it can score sixteen points (with a 6 Starter). And with a 3-4-5 Starter the hand will score fourteen. You must consider your discards if it's Jake's Crib. For example, a 3-4-5-6-10-10 hand, the proper discard would be a 3-10 (Jake's Crib).

As a general rule *do not hold this four-card run.* Hold the Ace-2-3 with a lone 9, 10, Jack, Queen, or King. Hold the 2-3-4 with a lone 6 or 8. A favorable Starter card can result in a fourteen point hand. In addition keeping a "Magic Eleven" and a "sleeper" will improve your pegging score. Your lead? The 3 is the percentage play.

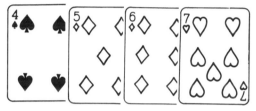

The 4-5-6-7 run is usually held as it also can score sixteen points (with a 4 Starter). But board position and discarding to Jake's Crib may force the four-card run to be abandoned.

This four-card run must be played with discretion. If it's your Crib discarding a 5 with a "ten" card may be your "percentage" play. Jake's lead? Keep the four-card run, especially if you're playing offense. Keep the 3-4-5 in combination with a 7 or 8, however, as this hand will score fourteen points with the "right" Starter. Check the board before making your discard decision.

If it's your Crib, break up this four-card run if you can discard the 5 with a "ten" card. The 6-7-8 held in combination with an Ace or 2 is especially desirable. The 5 in your Crib is the "percentage" play. Jake's Crib? Hold the four-card run. Again, check the board and your discards.

The 6-7-8-9 is usually left intact. A helping Starter card will score sixteen points. Your lead? The 8 is the percentage play, keeping the 6-7 for a possible "5-trap."

The 7-8-9-10 run is played with discretion. The 10 is discarded in many cases (for example, it's Jake's Crib and you hold 2-7-8-9-10-King. Discard the 10-King). Hold the basic 7-8-9 in combinations with the "Magic Eleven."

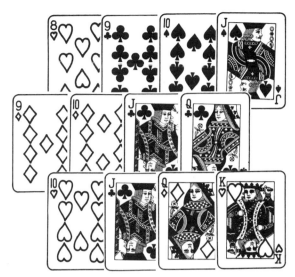

The percentage play for these combinations is to discard the high end of the run to Jake's Crib, and the low end of the run to your Crib. Try to hold a "Magic Eleven" combination. Of course, if the remaining two cards cannot help your hand, then hold the four-card run (example: 6-8-10-Jack-Queen-King, discard the 6-8). And as usual, board position plays a key role in making discarding decisions. You may want to discard defensively (8-King, for example).

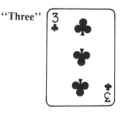

"Three"

"Thirteen"

Do I pair the Queen or play "fifteen-two"?

The percentage play is "fifteen-two." Jake probably holds "tens" and a 5 or 5's. By playing "fifteen-two," Jake will probably play another "ten" card for "twenty-five." This will be a "Go" and Jake will be forced to play a 5 if he has one. You then respond by leading your "safe" Queen. An excellent chance exists of a trap for a run of three. If you pair the Queen on your second play, you stand the risk of having your Jack trapped. Think ahead. Avoid traps and play the "percentage" play!

The End Game

More games are won or lost while Pegging those last few points than by all the astute play of the previous hands. Most *average* games are decided by five points or less. (Study the analysis' in Chapter Five). Pegging becomes critical, to say the least, in these games. There are some keys to defensive and offensive Pegging that should be basic to your game. Many of them have been covered earlier in the section on "Pegging Traps" and should be used in the end game when you're playing offensively. . .you need pegs to win!

Defensive Pegging

But let's start with defensive Pegging. Uncle Jake needs three pegs to win the game, and it's your lead (Jake's Crib). You are dealt Ace-4-4-6-7-King and need four points to win game. Keep the 4-4-7-King. The "Magic Eleven" is covered with the 7-4 combination. You have kept a small pair (4-4) to lead from, giving Jake only two chances to pair your lead card. The King gives you a safe "out" card. If Jake plays a 10-card on your 4 lead, for "fourteen," you play the safe King for "twenty-four." Jake's odds of scoring a "thirty-one" with a 7 are cut 25% because you are holding one of the 7's. Of course, if Jake does pair the 4 lead the game is over as you score pairs royal for six points and win the game.

This was an easy example. Many times you will not be dealt such ideal cards. The rule to remember in defensive Pegging is to always try to lead *a card smaller than a 5, preferably from a pair*. "Dump" your lone Jack at a safe opportunity, and always play the percentage play. Count the cards that can beat you and play accordingly. Don't play hunches!

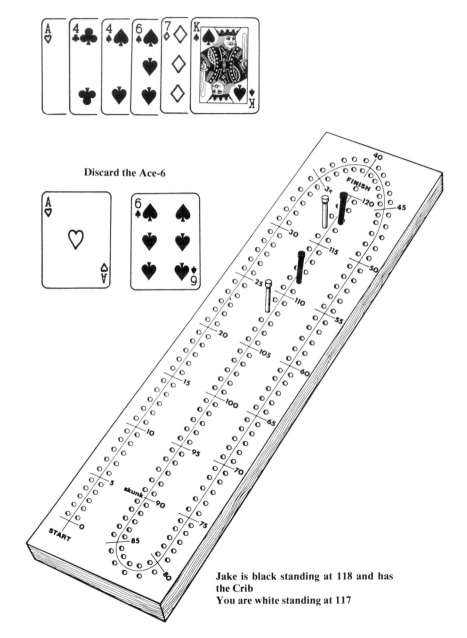

Discard the Ace-6

Jake is black standing at 118 and has the Crib
You are white standing at 117

The one exception to the percentage play: you have a lone 4 (or any lone small card) and were dealt a four-card combination of 6-9 or 7-8 (6-6-6-9, 6-6-9-9, 6-9-9-9, 7-7-7-8, 7-7-8-8, 7-8-8-8) leaving three cards to beat the 4 lead, and four cards to beat the 6,7,8, or 9 lead. Despite the one card disadvantage of leading from the 6,7,8, or 9, this is the percentage play, as any good player (especially Jake) will keep all small cards dealt to him, knowing this will be your logical play. If Jake is dealt an Ace-2-3-4-7-King, the 7-King will be discarded. For this reason when counting your losers in a desperation defense, if a 6 or higher card is a loser by *only* one more card . . . lead it! If the 6 or higher card will be beaten two more times? Don't do it! Lead the small card. The law of averages will bite you sooner or later playing hunches.

Another defensive tip. . .Jake needs four or more pegs to win the game. Don't get caught with one small card with the count above "twenty-one." You may be trapped into a run. Either dump a lone small card in the Crib, or better yet, play it early in the peg sequence to avoid a trap. And if Jake needs five or more points from the peg to win the game, don't get trapped with 4-5-6 cards as your last Pegging card. Get rid of these potential losers. Especially the 5. If Jake needs seven or more points, the 5 held to the last card can indeed be deadly. . .being trapped into a 4-5-6 combination, or a 5-5-5 situation.

Good defensive Pegging comes with practice. Study your opponent; learn his habits. Does he always lead a 4 to a 9? Is he aggressive? Does he always lead from a pair if possible, or does he commonly hold a pair for last? Study his habits and it may be a game-saver in a tight spot. But once again, don't play hunches!

These observations should be used *only* when a decision has to be made between cards that have *equal* odds of being beaten. And use logic. Think. Remember your discards. Consider the starter card.

Jake will *attempt* to keep these cards . . .

. . . when Pegging will decide the game

Nevertheless, an Ace, 2, 3, or 4 is your percentage lead (see the probability chart on the next page)

Probability of Jake Scoring on Your First Card Played (Pegging is Critical)

Jake will have these preferences when Pegging is critical:

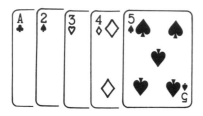

Strong Preference

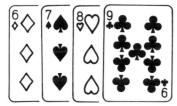

Some Preference

Slight Preference

No Preference

What are the odds of Jake (dealer) scoring on your first Pegging card played? Despite the strong preference Jake will have for the Ace, 2, 3, or 4, your odds in defensive Pegging dictate your leading them, if possible (see chart).

Pegging Odds

Of the six cards dealt to you *and* the Starter card you have seen:	Your First Play	Percent Loser Pegging Critical	Percent Loser Pegging Not Critical
One 4 (or one Ace, 2, or 3)	4 (or Ace, 2, 3)	42%*	28%
Two 4's (or two Aces, 2's, 3's)	4 (or Ace, 2, 3)	28%	19%
Three 4's (or three Aces, 2's, 3's)	4 (or Ace, 2, 3)	14%	9%
Four 4's (or four Aces, 2's, 3's)	4 (or Ace, 2, 3)	0%	0%
One 6 or 9	6 or 9	65%**	55%**
Two 6-9 combination (6-6, 6-9, 9-9)	6 or 9	60%	50%
Three 6-9 combination	6 or 9	55%	45%
Four 6-9 combination	6 or 9	47%	37%
Five 6-9 combination	6 or 9	42%	28%
Six 6-9 combination	6 or 9	28%	19%
Seven 6-9 combination	6 or 9		
7-8 combination odds same as 6-9			
One 10-Jack-Queen-King	10-J-Q or K	60%	50%
Two 10-Jack-Queen-King-5 (J-5)	10-J-Q or K	55%***	45%
Three 10-Jack-Queen-King-5 (J-J-5, J-5-5)	10-J-Q or K	50%	40%
Four 10-Jack-Queen-King-5	10-J-Q or K	45%	35%
Five 10-Jack-Queen-King-5	10-J-Q or K	35%	25%
Six 10-Jack-Queen-King-5	10-J-Q or K	25%	15%
Seven 10-Jack-Queen-King-5	10-J-Q or K	10%	5%

*Formula (three 4's are outstanding among 45 unknown cards): $3/45 + 3/44 + 3/43 + 3/42 + 3/41 + 3/40 = 42\%$
**Empirical knowledge
***Assumes one 5 has been seen. Lower percent if 2 or more 5's have been seen

Offensive Pegging

Offensive Pegging: you need pegs to beat Uncle Jake. This situation takes guile to beat the good player. Leading from a small pair may *not* be the effective lead. Even leading from a small card may not be the best lead. Entice the play; control the cards that Uncle Jake can play safely. Lead your "sleeper" card. Camouflage your hand. Work the traps. Keep two cards for last that will count for you (a pair or two cards that add to fifteen). If counters can't be held for last, keep two cards that could combine into a run (with luck).

Know your opponent's habits. If you know Jake plays a 9, if possible, on 4 leads when you are playing desperation offense, and you have a 4 and 9, then, of course, play the 4! And pair the 9!

If you need six or more points Pegging to win game, you need the luck of the deal. The best way to peg six or more is with a pair of small cards—Aces or Deuces preferably. Try to work a trap with the count past twenty-one. For example, you are dealt Ace-Ace-8-9-Jack-Queen. Keep the Ace-Ace-8-9. You must hope for a "ten" card lead, and depending on whether you need four pegs or six, play your 9 (you need four pegs) or your 8 (you need six pegs). A good player like Uncle Jake will be extremely hard to trap, but an average player can be nailed from time to time. If you are not fortunate to be dealt a small pair in this situation, then concentrate on trapping your opponent into long runs, or keeping *any* pair for your last two cards in a desperate try for a trap for pairs royal. Jacks work best for this trap. See the diagrams for more tips on Pegging the end game.

Jake will be playing defense . . . lead the "sleeper" 2

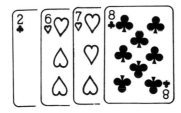 

Jake has a defensive habit of playing a 9 on a 4 lead. If you entice a 9, your 2 will score a "fifteen-two"

 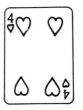

End Game Pegging

Your lead (Jake's Crib)
You both need three
points to win the game

This is a subtle hand. Discard the 9-Jack. Lead the 8 in an attempt to entice a 7 (53% chance). Your 6 then wins the game. Another option is to hold the 5-6-9-Queen and lead the Queen in hopes of enticing a 5. Enticing a 5 has only a 40% chance of succeeding—13% less than enticing a 7 (holding the 5-6-8-Queen and leading the 8). And even if you were successful in enticing a 5, Jake would probably get the "Go" and win the game.

Discard the 10-King (this hand illustrates the unfavorable bias for "ten" cards when Pegging is of prime importance). Lead the 3. Jake's chances of pairing the 3 are 27% (you have seen two 3's). And if Jake has a 3 for "six," your 9 will score "fifteen-two."

Discard the Queens. Lead the 7. If Jake pairs the 7, your Ace will score "fifteen-two." If Jake plays an 8 on your 7 lead, your 6 will form a run of three and the game is yours. The chances of Jake having a 7 or 8? 80% (less the slight bias shown these cards).

Discard the 7-King of clubs (you can fake a flush with the King of hearts). Lead the King of hearts in an attempt to entice a 5 (27% chance). If successful, pair Jake's 5 and hope to get the "Go" and the game with your Ace. The odds of Jake having the third 5? A meager 13%.

72

Jake's lead (your Crib)

Discard the Queen-King. Pair Jake's lead if possible. The 3 is your "safe" card (the Starter card cuts Jake's chances of having a 3). Entice any play that you can retaliate for two points.

Discard the 7-Jack. The Ace-2-4 are key cards in this situation. You must Peg at least three points. As the dealer you are assured at least one point. The 9 is held in preference to the 7 as it will run the count nearer thirty-one, increasing your odds of scoring with your small cards. Of course, the 2-9 forms the "Magic Eleven" and will stop any "ten" leads. You will be forced to gamble and pair Jake's lead, if possible. The unbiased odds of Jake scoring pairs royal are 27%; however, Jake will be leading an extremely biased selection (if he has a pair, that will almost certainly be his lead). But the risk must be taken . . . pair away.

Discard two 6's. Play the 10 on any of Jake's logical Ace-2-3-4 leads. If he responds with a "fifteen-two," then play your Jack. With luck that will be a "Go" and your lone 6 will score "thirty-one." Then hope for a "ten" lead. And if Jake's first lead is a "ten," play your 5 for two points.

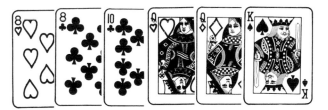

Ouch! This is a terrible Pegging hand. Your best chances are of holding a pair for last, hoping to play them back to back for three points. Discard the 10-King. Normally you would keep cards to cover as many of Jake's as possible, but the "ten" card bias cuts the odds too low for pairing a 10 or King.

This is an ideal Pegging hand. Discard the 8-Jack. If Jake leads from small cards, play the 9. If he leads from middle cards, play the King. And if he leads a "ten" card (Jack-Queen-King), play the 9. If a 10 is led, play the King. Keep the Aces for a back to back pair to win the game.

Cribbage Psychology

We all know that people are creatures of habit. And Cribbage players are no different. Old *Homo sapiens* just keeps doing the same thing over and over. It's amazing how habitually we dress, eat, sleep, talk. . .it's just more comfortable to do "our thing" the same old way. Certainly, it's more exciting to do something new, but the facts are, we rarely do. And the older we are, the less apt we are to do something new.

The same is true of Cribbage players. They get in a groove, a pattern. They consistently make the same plays, use the same mannerisms, the same voice inflections, and play at the same speed. Study your opponent. If you play Jake a hundred games, you should know what every little mannerism means, what typical cards are followed by another card. You should know if he is an aggressive player, or a conservative player (incidentally, an aggressive player will beat a conservative player by about 2%, skill levels being equal).

Some typical mannerisms that can predict a play or a situation are:

- In a friendly game, Jake discards to the Crib, (and despite the rules) takes a quick second look at his discards. More than likely it means that three of his remaining cards are of one suit and he wants to make sure he isn't discarding a flush opportunity. If he changes discards, play him for a flush; if he *doesn't* change discards, ignore a flush fake.

- You lead the first card and Jake takes a few extra seconds to respond. The odds are he is debating whether to pair the lead or not. If he does *not* pair the lead, lay a trap for this card.

- An average player has two cards left to play and hesitates slightly before playing. He is *not* leading from a pair. You can safely pair his lead. Of course, this slip is seldom made by good players. Continue to pair this "hesitation" lead until your opponent wises up to his mistake, and traps you with a "hesitation pitch" when leading from a pair! Conversely, many good players will give you the "hesitation" pitch *only* when leading from a pair. The "expert" analyzes his opponent and chooses the method that works most consistently.

- Your opponent has two cards remaining, and plays one without any apparent thought. This may be a careless play. The odds are good that your opponent is leading from a pair.

- Your opponent runs the count to twenty-seven with an Ace. You have an Ace and a 4-card but are unsure of taking the risk of pairing the Ace (giving your opponent the chance of a pairs royal) or taking the "safe" thirty-one play with the 4. Hesitate for a second or two, faking a "Go." In a fast game, your opponent may instinctively reach for his peg, giving away the fact that he does *not* have another ace (or any other small card, for that matter). Then you can safely pair the Ace, gaining an extra point.

- You play an Ace to make the count twenty-seven. You have no other small cards and you want to prevent Jake from pairing your Ace. Fake another small card by *not* making a move for your pegs, *and* by subtly starting to pull another card from your hand. This could convince Jake you are holding another Ace, and he'll play a safer card, saving a point or two.

• Some players carelessly let their emotions give their hands away. They bubble over with enthusiasm when they have good fortune, and pout glumly when they have a poor hand. Watch for any telltale mannerisms, especially immediately after turning up the Starter card. It's amazing how poorly players mask their emotions.

These are just a few of hundreds of possible mannerisms to look for. Study your opponent for every possible clue to his play. You'll be amazed what a creature of habit he (or she) is.

On the other hand, make every effort to keep your game from becoming too predictable. Play at the same speed as possible for all plays. At times you must take an extra second or two to make a decision. Try to duplicate this mannerism when you *don't* have a tough decision to make. From time to time, hesitate a bit (not too obvious, though, keep it subtle) when leading from a pair (your last two cards). Remember, your speed of play can be a big clue to Jake. Keep your hand (and your feelings) camouflaged.

And speaking of camouflaging your hand with your mannerisms, keep your hand camouflaged *visually*, too! Some players get in the habit of arranging their cards high-to-low, left-to-right (or vice versa). A sharp player will pick this up. If, for example, you arrange your cards with the high cards to the left, and you play a 7, pulling it from the first spot on the right, old Jake will know you don't have any cards smaller than a 7.

You've seen a good poker player in action. Notice how he squeezes his cards for a look-see, and holds them in the palm of his hand so that opposing players cannot see his cards. That's not bad advice for Cribbage players, too. This is especially true when playing a stranger in a tournament. He may be a sharpie, the cards may be marked, or he may pick up a mannerism in the way you arrange your cards. One less clue, the better.

Speaking of marked cards, the danger always exists of your opponent cheating. The less said of this the better, since Cribbage is a sporting game and has no room for cheaters. However, the ugly truth is a few players cheat. Watch for marked cards, "short" decks (fewer than 52 cards), crimped cards, "shiners" (reflective surfaced items), kibitzers who may give signals, dealing from the bottom of the deck, or "sneaking a peek."

If you suspect cheating by manipulating the deck, the rules give you (the nondealer) an opportunity to shuffle first. This will make it tougher to manipulate the deck, but makes for an extremely awkward game. The best solution is simply *not* play with a suspected cheater. And, of course, *always* check to see if the peg is accurate. Even an honest player will make a mistake in Pegging. . .and it's amazing how often it's in his favor. If this happens too often, insist on the "muggins" rule, and this form of cheating will suddenly come to an end!

Ah ha! Nothing smaller than a 7!

Gobble . . .

Gobble

Gooble

Turkey Plays

Some standard plays in Cribbage occur rather consistently, and are misplayed by many players. Some are *Big* turkey plays (rather obvious to a good player) and some are *Little* turkey plays—mistakes that aren't too obvious and are misplayed by good players, too. Study the diagrams. There will be some arguments, or disagreements, with the *Little* turkey plays. . .but that's what Cribbage is all about. A friendly fast-paced game with millions of options! Perhaps you can come up with better solutions. Most of these "turkey" plays have been analyzed through hundreds of thousands of hands and are based upon empirical knowledge. . .and the school of hard knocks! What may work 49 times will lose 51 times. . .and it takes years of experience to know which plays work the most often.

Big Turkey Plays

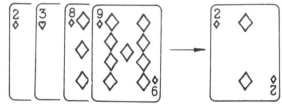

The 2 lead is a "turkey" play for two reasons. First, the play is not covered if Jake pairs the 2. Second, it probably will not draw a desired "ten" card response. The 3 is the play. The 9 backs the play for a "fifteen-two" if Jake pairs the 3 lead. The 3 will be answered with a "ten" card more often than will a 2 lead.

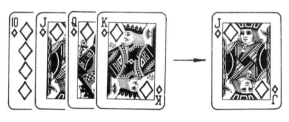

Double gobble, gobble! A Jack is the most likely "ten" card held by Jake. And you have no card covering your play.

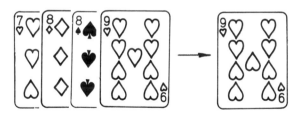

Another bone-head play. If Jake plays a logical 6 on the 9 lead, you're in big trouble. The correct play is leading from strength—one of the 8's. Your play is then covered and you remain in the driver's seat.

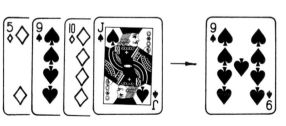

Again, the 9 lead is not backed by a retaliatory card. Play the 10 and the odds are you'll trade points. Your third card should then be the 9, not the Jack (if Jake played a 5 on the 10 lead).

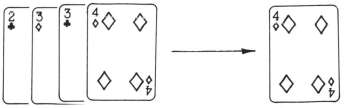

Leading a lone 9 to a lone 6 is a no-no. If Jakes plays a 6 for "fifteen-two," and you retaliate with your 6 for "twenty-one," the possibility exists of Jake having the third 6 for pairs royal. Lead the lone 6 to the lone 9.

Leading the lone 4 is a gross mistake. It covers only Jake's 2, 3, 5, 8 and 9. The correct lead is the 3. It covers the Ace, 2, 3, 4, 5, 8, 9, 10, Jack, Queen, and King.

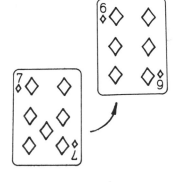

Pairing Jake's Queen instead of playing a 5 for "fifteen-two" could cost you a bundle of peg points. If Jake has a 5, and paired your first 5, the chances are excellent for your scoring pairs royal *and* a following "thirty-one" with the 6.

Playing the 6 on Jake's 7 lead gives Jake a chance at a free run of three with a retaliatory 5. Playing a 9 on the 7 gives Jake no better than a trade of points if he scores with another 9 for a pair (your 6 follows for "thirty-one"). If Jake decides to form a run of three with an 8, your 6 follows for a run of four and a probable "Go" and a profit of two points.

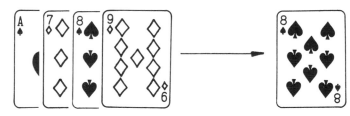

Leading the 2 is a "turkey" play for two reasons. First, the play is not covered in the event Jake pairs it, and second, the 2 will not entice a 9 as readily as the 4. The 4 is the correct lead. The 4 is backed by the 7 if Jake pairs it. If Jakes responds with the logical 9, your 2 scores a "fifteen-two."

Oops! If Jakes pairs the 8 lead you cannot recoup your two points. Lead the 7 and if Jake pairs it, your ace recovers the two points with a "fifteen-two."

Little Turkey Plays

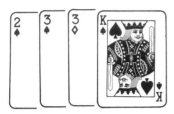 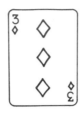

The 3 is the correct lead, but the flush fake opportunity has escaped. Lead the *3 of spades*.

Oops. Leading the 7 will give Jake that slim opportunity for double pairs royal (if he also has a pair of 7's). Leading an 8 takes away that chance.

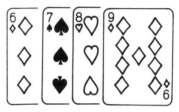 

The King is a poor lead. A slim hope of pairing a 10 exists with the King lead, but leading the 2 (the correct lead) gives you the chance of pairing a 10-Queen-King (three cards vs. the one card opportunity the King lead offers).

This is one of the most common mistakes Cribbage players make. Leading the 7 allows the 5-trap to escape, and, in addition, allows "ten"-5 combinations to get the "Go." The correct lead is the 8, keeping a 5-trap try intact *and* if Jake plays a following "ten" card, the 9 runs the counts to "twenty-seven," getting the "Go" if Jake has a 5.

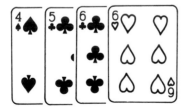 

Playing offensively, the 4 is a poor lead. The chance of a high-scoring 5-trap can be collected if Jake is holding 5-"tens," and you lead a 6. Jake would be forced to play "sixteen," followed by your second 6 for "twenty-two." Jake's 5 would then be forced into play for "twenty-seven," followed by your 4 for "thirty-one" and a run of three for 5 big points. And it's amazing how often this works. However, if you're playing defensively, the 4 is a good lead.

Playing offensively, the Queen is a poor lead, as it forces the 10-Jack-King off the play, minimizing your chances of scoring three or four points with your Aces. Leading the 9 entices a Queen-King response, and if successful, your following Queen (for a pair if good fortune is smiling on you) runs the count to "twenty-nine." This gives you an excellent opportunity for playing your Aces back to back for four points. Playing defensively? Lead an Ace (the diamond).

78

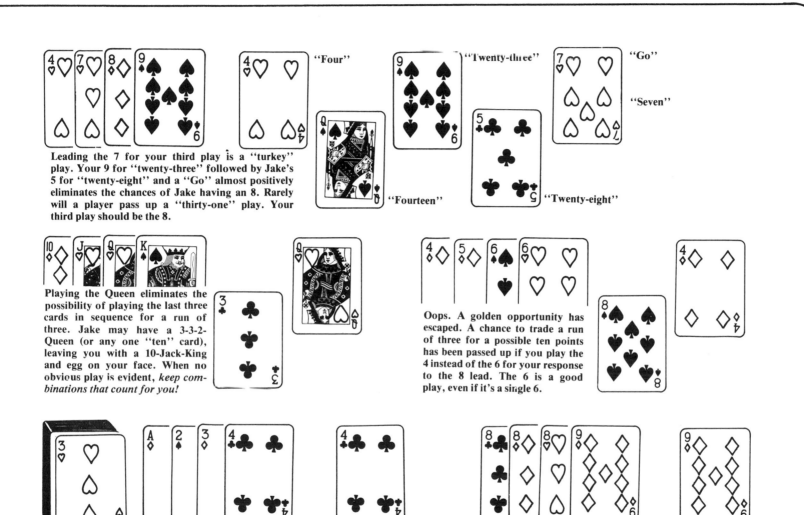

Leading the 7 for your third play is a "turkey" play. Your 9 for "twenty-three" followed by Jake's 5 for "twenty-eight" and a "Go" almost positively eliminates the chances of Jake having an 8. Rarely will a player pass up a "thirty-one" play. Your third play should be the 8.

Playing the Queen eliminates the possibility of playing the last three cards in sequence for a run of three. Jake may have a 3-3-2-Queen (or any one "ten" card), leaving you with a 10-Jack-King and egg on your face. When no obvious play is evident, *keep combinations that count for you!*

Oops. A golden opportunity has escaped. A chance to trade a run of three for a possible ten points has been passed up if you play the 4 instead of the 6 for your response to the 8 lead. The 6 is a good play, even if it's a single 6.

Leading the 4 when the Starter card is a 3 is a critical boner, especially if end-game Pegging is involved. The 4 stands a 40% chance of being paired. The 3 cuts the odds of being paired to 27% (end-game: no bias). The odds are a little less of this being a losing play early in the game. The 3 covers any "ten" response, as does the 4. Play the 3.

There's absolutely no advantage to leading a 9 here, saving three 8's. It is mathematically impossible to play the three 8's in sequence. As a rule, always *lead* from three of a kind (exception: three Aces, 2's, 3's with a lone 9 or a lone "ten" card).

79

Cribbage for the Expert

Now that you know how to run traps, play offense, play defense, fake flushes, dump Jacks, entice the play, use psychological tricks, apply logic, and have a solid end game. . .what's left to learn? How can my game be improved to insure winning. . .even against an expert player?

Remember what Lord Kelvin said way back in the 19th Century:

> ". . .that when you can measure what you are speaking about, and express it in numbers, you know something about it; but when you cannot express it in numbers, your knowledge is of a meager and unsatisfactory kind."

To carry this thought a bit further, can you honestly say that you can play the first card of the very first hand with absolute certainty? And the second card? In fact, can you play the entire hand with absolute certainty? Do you know when to "play on"? When to "play off"? If not, your knowledge of Cribbage *IS* of a meager and unsatisfactory kind!

Suppose you're the nondealer. Your very first hand consists of the 4-5-Queen-King. Do you know the correct card to lead? The 4? No. The correct card to open the game is the King.

You're the dealer and your first hand consists of the 4-5-6-King. Your opponent leads a King. Do you know the correct response? The 5 for fifteen-two? Pair the King? No. The correct play is the 6. Both the King led by the nondealer, and the 6 response by the dealer are made with absolute certainty.

But wait, earlier in this book, leading from a card lower than a 5 was recommended as the percentage play. . .the play with 57% less chance of your opponent scoring. And for the dealer, if the King is led, why not play a 5 for fifteen-two or at least pair the King? Why lay off?

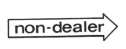  

Lead the King?

And respond with 6?

The "Twenty-six Theory"

An explanation of these controversial plays will come later. But first, I have developed a mathematical method of play that has been tried and proven, with thousands of games charted, tens of thousands of hands analyzed, and the results thoroughly studied. During this study, a method of play slowly evolved. . . a theory of play. A theory I have named the "Twenty-six Theory."

This "Twenty-six Theory," if played consistently, will improve your winning average a full 6%. Insignificant, you're thinking. But in this tough, subtle game of Cribbage 6% is the winning edge. Beating Uncle Jake by 6% is quite an achievement! Of course, players of lesser skill will fall at a much higher rate. By applying the "Twenty-six Theory" your winning average will bound upwards against players of all skill levels. The "Twenty-six Theory," the ultimate Cribbage weapon! The weapon that tells you exactly what card to play. . .when to play it, almost without exception.

Remember the old "Law of Averages"? That Law that has built the gambling empires, creating fortunes for the gambling houses? The Law that beats you at Roulette, beats you at the dice table, beats you at the Black Jack tables? This same Law can work for you at Cribbage, too. A Law of Averages operates in Cribbage, just as surely as it operates in any other card game.

But Cribbage is a subtle card game. . .in fact, one of the most subtle card games devised by man. Players learn the basics quickly, and become competitive quickly. So quickly, in fact, that in a 121-point game, average players are actually dueling over the ten points or so (and usually much less) that can actually be controlled by the players, and not controlled by the luck of the draw. This small edge makes playing the "average" that much more important. Every point earned, or lost, through skillful, or unskillful play is critical to winning consistently. . .or losing consistently. And this is where the "Twenty-six Theory" comes in.

After compiling and averaging thousands of hands I found that the average points scored and pegged by the nondealer is 10.2. This same compiling and averaging gives the dealer (including Pegging and scoring the Crib) 16.2 points per deal. Every *two* deals, the average points add to 26.4. This is the basis of the Cribbage Law of Averages. And hence the name of my theory.

Now, let's project these average points per deal around the 121-point board. First, the nondealer: 10.2, 26.4, 36.6, 52.8, 63.0, 79.2, 89.4, 105.6, and on the ninth deal stands at 115.8.

Now, the average points per deal for the dealer (remember, he has the *first* Crib): 16.2, 26.4, 42.6, 52.8, 69.0, 79.2, 95.4, 105.6, and on the ninth deal stands at 121.8.

The Cribbage Law of Averages says the dealer will win the game by scoring his Crib hand on the ninth deal. The nondealer will be about five (5.2) points short after counting first on the ninth hand. And this crucial five points will, *on the average*, cause the nondealer to lose fifty-six games of 100 (skill levels being equal, of course). These averages are the foundation of the "Twenty-six Theory."

The "Twenty-six Theory" uses "Twenty-six" as the *average* rather than "twenty-seven" (dropping the .4) because it's easier to slow a game (play off) than it is to speed up (play on) the game. It takes both players' cooperation to form runs, "Fifteen's", and pairs. However, if *one* player decides to play defense and lays off forming runs, pairs, and "fifteen's", his opponent is stymied.

So, with twenty-six as the basis for the theory, let's once again project the players around the 121-point board. First, the nondealer: 10, 26, 36, 52, 62, 78, 88, 104, and on the ninth hand, 114. *Seven* points short of game. Projecting the dealer: 16, 26, 42, 52, 68, 78, 94, 104, and on the ninth hand, 120. *One* point short of game.

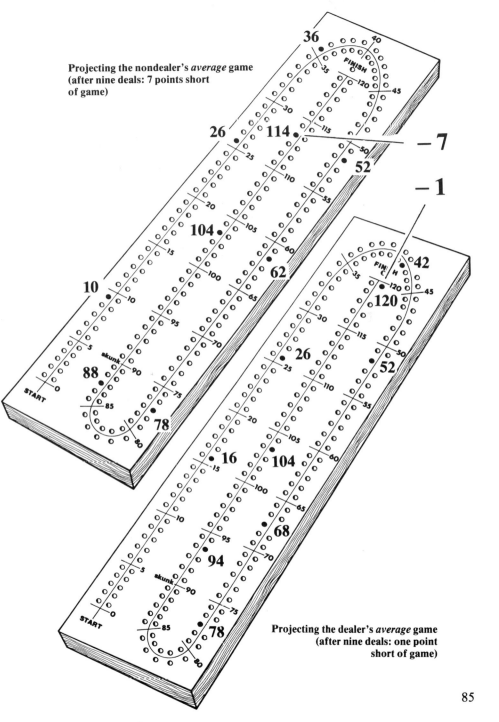

Projecting the nondealer's *average* game (after nine deals: 7 points short of game)

Projecting the dealer's *average* game (after nine deals: one point short of game)

Playing the "Twenty-six Theory," the dealer has the commanding edge in an *average* game, standing at 120 points after nine hands. The dealer will have *first* count on the tenth hand, and in control of the game. The average game gives the dealer the commanding edge. . .the winning edge. Of course, the odds of playing an absolute average game are astronomical, but nevertheless, this average—the Cribbage Law of Averages—gives the dealer of the first hand the edge.

Well, you're thinking, so the odds are with me when I deal the first hand, and the odds are against me when I'm the nondealer on the first hand. How do I pick up that extra 6% in winnings?

Once again, using the "Twenty-six Theory," after nine *average* hands are completed, the nondealer is *seven* points short of game. Seven tough points to peg on the tenth hand. The dealer, however, is one point short of game after counting his ninth hand and Crib, needing but a single peg on the tenth hand, *and* has *first* count. . .a simple matter to win the game.

Playing to this average, the basic strategy of the game becomes apparent. **The nondealer must play offense with his very first card played in the game. The dealer must play defense with his very first card played in the game.** Why? The nondealer must pick up an additional seven points over average during the nine-hand game to gain the advantage. And, of course, the more points picked up over *average,* the better. Being seven or more points over average, *and* having the first count on the ninth hand is the goal of the nondealer.

The dealer, on the other hand, must play defense—slow the game down—to insure counting *first* on the tenth hand. The dealer has nine points (plus-nine), he

can *sacrifice* to defense and still maintain his advantage. Remember, after counting his hand and Crib on the ninth hand, he is *one* point short of 121, and will *average* ten points on the tenth hand (nondealer's average ten points per deal).

Starting the game. . .

Of course, as stated earlier, a game rarely, if ever, runs exactly average around the board. Adjustments must be made as the score fluctuates during the game. A player may begin (as the dealer) playing defense, but may be forced into playing offense on the very next hand (if his first hand was a complete bust, scoring seven points or less). His strategy may swing back to defense later in the game if he scores a "barn-burner," or if the game progresses at an extremely slow pace.

About one game in ten will run approximately average for the entire game. These are the games you must win! Whether you are the dealer or the nondealer on the first hand, these average games are yours. And this is your winning edge. These are the games the "Twenty-six Theory" will win for you.

The non-average games will be won by the lucky recipient of the good cards. . .the good cuts for the Starter card (skill levels being equal). And as for these non-average games, the Law of Averages will come through for you (sooner or later). You will win your share of these games. Of course you will win more of these non-average games if you are the more skillful player, and less if your opponent is the more skilled.

But getting back to the average games, the "Twenty-six Theory" will give you the 6% edge playing an "expert". . .and a much greater edge against the average player. Against a beginner, it's downright devastating, with edges up to 50% or more (winning 75 of 100 games) not uncommon.

Let's begin a game with you being the nondealer. Your objective is to speed up the game, to play offense. . .to gain those seven points over average to give you the advantage on the ninth hand.

Being the nondealer, you, of course, discard to the dealer's Crib on the first deal. *Contrary* to what was taught early in the book ("Beginning Cribbage"), don't be *overly* concerned with balking the Crib. Hold your hand to score *maximum* count. . .even at the expense of giving Uncle Jake a good Crib. If Uncle Jake does get a high-scoring Crib on the first deal, he still must make up seventeen tough points over average *to count first and win on the eighth hand* (the dealer stands at 94 after seven average hands, and with first count on the eighth hand, scoring an average ten points, will be at 104 points. . . seventeen points short of winning the game).

After discarding, and holding cards to form maximum count, begin Pegging by leading a card that will entice a score, and allow you to retaliate with a score. Even if it means risking a pairs royal. . .or coming out on the short end of a run, SCORE! Take every pair, every run, every "fifteen" possible!

Go! Go! Go!

nondealer

Early in the game. . .

Getting back to Lord Kelvin and the example of the 4-5-Queen-King. The King is led! Why? The most likely card held by Jake will be a 5. The least likely "ten" card held by Jake will be a King. By leading the King, your chances of scoring are best. You hope to entice a 5 from Jake for "fifteen-two" and you counter with your 5 for a pair and two points. Even if Jake defies the odds and has the third 5 for pairs royal, running the count to twenty-five, your 4 will probably gain the "Go." You have scored three badly needed points. . .and even if Jake had the third 5, and pegged eight points on the exchange, he is still far short of the seventeen he needs to gain to win the game with first count on the eighth hand (if the game progresses approximately average).

Leading the 4 from the 4-5-Queen-King hand may draw a King or Queen that you could pair for two points, running the count to twenty-four, without much chance of a followup for thirty-one or a "Go." But the odds are for a lower peg score, resulting in you not picking up many of those seven points (minus-seven) over average you need to gain the advantage. PLAY THE CARD THAT WILL RESULT IN THE MOST PEG POINTS POSSIBLE. . . REGARDLESS OF THE NUMBER OF PEGS YOUR OPPONENT SCORES!

If you are the dealer, the first hand should be played defensively. Your major objective is to hold your opponent *scoreless* on the peg. Lay *off* his lead; do *not* form runs, be extremely cautious about counting to fifteen. . .especially on the first card lead. Keep cards to form the "Magic Eleven" to thwart the 10-card lead. . .even if it weakens the count in your hand—PLAY DEFENSIVELY! Pat yourself on the back if Jake fails to peg a point on the first hand. . . you have done your duty. Remember, you can give up nine points (you are plus-nine) and still have the advantage in an average game.

And once again, returning to old Lord Kelvin and knowing your numbers, if Jake leads a King and you're holding 4-5-6-King, resist that temptation to play your 5 for a "fifteen-two." Doubly resist the temptation to pair the King—a pairs royal retaliation may very well be fatal! The play is for the 6 for sixteen, keeping the 5 (the other half of the "Magic Eleven") to score thirty-one in the case of the logical 10-card followup by Jake—resulting in only two points for you, but, more importantly, NO points for Jake. Continue to play defensively the remainder of the pegging on the first hand.

The only exception to this rule is if you have an extremely bad hand (two points or less. . .and the discards you have laid away in your Crib are *not* helped by the Starter card, with the possibility that you have, indeed, lost your plus-nine advantage on the very first hand). In this event, peg cautiously, and score when you get no worse than a trade. Be especially cautious if Uncle Jake's first lead will combine with the Starter card into a possible "barnburner." Before trading points on the peg, check his second card played. If it also combines with the Starter card, avoid Pegging, as a twelve or higher hand, plus a few pegs, will certainly put Jake in the driver's seat! If his third card played does not combine with the Starter card, collect Pegging points—but cautiously! There will, of course, be times when you have no alternative but to go ahead and peg, being trapped into a situation with no safe cards. Take your lumps, but keep them to a minimum.

Scoring throughout the game by the first-hand's nondealer is more critical to the outcome of the game than is the scoring of the first-hand's dealer. Statistics show that the average game is nine hands (see the following chapter). The nondealer scores first on this critical ninth hand and, after scoring, is about seven points short of winning the game (in a typically average game). One big hand (sixteen or more) scored during one of the nine hands will pick up those minus-seven points, providing the other eight hands are about average.

However, the dealer must score at least *two* big hands (sixteen or more) to gain the minus-seventeen points he must pick up to win the game with FIRST COUNT on the EIGHTH HAND! Picking up minus-seventeen in eight hands is much more difficult for the dealer than is picking up minus-seven points by the nondealer in nine hands.

For this reason, the nondealer's score is usually the key to the game. The dealer must make early efforts to slow the game down—to make the game ten hands. Or at least force the nondealer to be no better than average, and as far below average as possible, by playing defensively throughout the game (or until board position dictates a shift in strategy). And, of course, the nondealer must make every effort to speed the game—to make the game nine hands, and being in position (less than ten points from the 121st hole) to take advantage of that ninth-hand first count.

Since the nondealer's position throughout the game is usually more critical than the dealer's position, let's analyze the nondealer's strategy. First, let's plot the board with marks, or targets to shoot for on each hand. This is the primary reason for playing with an easy to read 121-point board. Since you must pick up seven points over average to be in first-count range of winning the game on the critical ninth hand, let's add seven points to the locations you should be during an average game. Set your goal for seventeen as "par" on the first deal, then thirty-three as par on deal two, then forty-three, fifty-nine, sixty-nine, eighty-five, ninety-five, and finally 111 as "par" after completing the eighth deal.

The nondealer's par holes

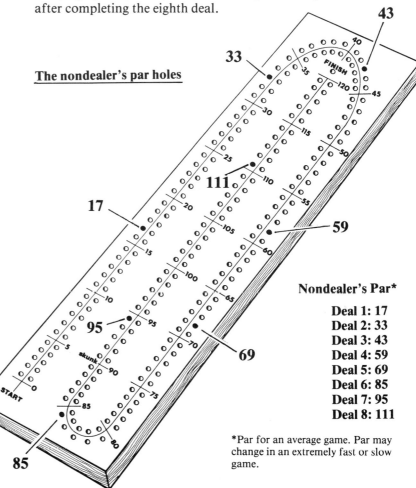

Nondealer's Par*

Deal 1: 17
Deal 2: 33
Deal 3: 43
Deal 4: 59
Deal 5: 69
Deal 6: 85
Deal 7: 95
Deal 8: 111

*Par for an average game. Par may change in an extremely fast or slow game.

Then, through playing offensively throughout the game, if you have attained or exceeded "par" 111 after playing the eighth deal, the odds of winning the game are in your favor. You are within ten points of winning the game with first count, and the odds are even you will score at least ten points as the non-dealer on the ninth hand. Of course, many games will NOT be average, but a compilation of statistics shows that about 42% of all games *are decided on the ninth hand*. Study the charts in the next chapter, "What's the Odds?" and you will understand why the ninth deal is so important in Cribbage!

If you attain the "par" 111th hole after the eighth deal, you still have only a 50-50 chance of winning the game (if Uncle Jake has maintained the pace with you). Still, 50-50 is better than losing those 12%, if the "Twenty-six Theory" isn't played. But try to surpass the "par" points by as many plus points as possible. With each point on the plus side of "par," your odds of winning increase.

For example, if you have scored thirty-six points after deal two, you are plus-three to "par." If Jake, the dealer of the first hand, is tied with you at thirty-six points after the second deal, he is minus-seven to "par." Confusing? This minus-seven means he is seven points under "par" to score 121 on *first count on the eighth deal*. The dealer of the first hand must *speed up the game one full hand* to gain that first count advantage (or, if successful in slowing the game, will have that critical first-count advantage on the tenth hand). The first hand dealer's target, or "par" for the second hand would be forty-three (your third hand target).

The dealer's par holes

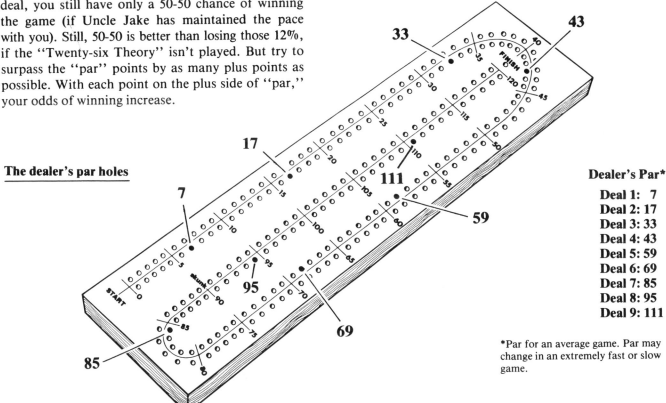

Dealer's Par*

Deal 1: 7
Deal 2: 17
Deal 3: 33
Deal 4: 43
Deal 5: 59
Deal 6: 69
Deal 7: 85
Deal 8: 95
Deal 9: 111

*Par for an average game. Par may change in an extremely fast or slow game.

These numbers will be confusing at first, but mastery of board position is critical to expert Cribbage. Don't give up at this point. Take your time and study the "par" numbers. Remember, the nondealer will have first count on ODD NUMBERED deals, the dealer will have first count on EVEN NUMBERED deals. And although the average game is nine deals, many games will go eight or ten deals. A few games will be won in seven or eleven deals. About one game in 300 will be won in six deals. . . with a twelve-deal game not quite as rare. A thirteen-deal game is about a 1,000 to 1 shot. The shortest game recorded in some 25,000 games witnessed is a five-deal game! The reason longer games are not as rare as short games is that poor, low-counting, hands are more common than those high-counting "barn-burners" (suspicions confirmed?), and by the fact it is easier to slow a game down than to speed it up.

Let's play a typical game, hand by hand, deal by deal, and get the feel for playing the "Twenty-six Theory." Since the game usually revolves around the nondealer's score, let's analyze the game from that standpoint first.

Playing the "Twenty-six Theory"

Deal one. As the nondealer you are -7. Your par is 17.

Summary: as the nondealer, your objective is *maximum* score. By holding the 9 instead of the Queen you cover the 3 lead for maximum Pegging score (many players mistakenly discard the 9-King as balk-ing cards to Jake's Crib). Despite the nine peg points score by Jake, your total score of sixteen points (-1) vs. Jake's total of twenty-two points (three-point Crib) makes the game a virtual tossup. Jake is -11 for an eight-hand game try, but +15 for scoring first count on the tenth deal. Your score at this point is the key to the game. -1 to average for winning on the ninth deal (with first count).

Deal one. Your score: 16 (-1). Jake's score: 22(-11).

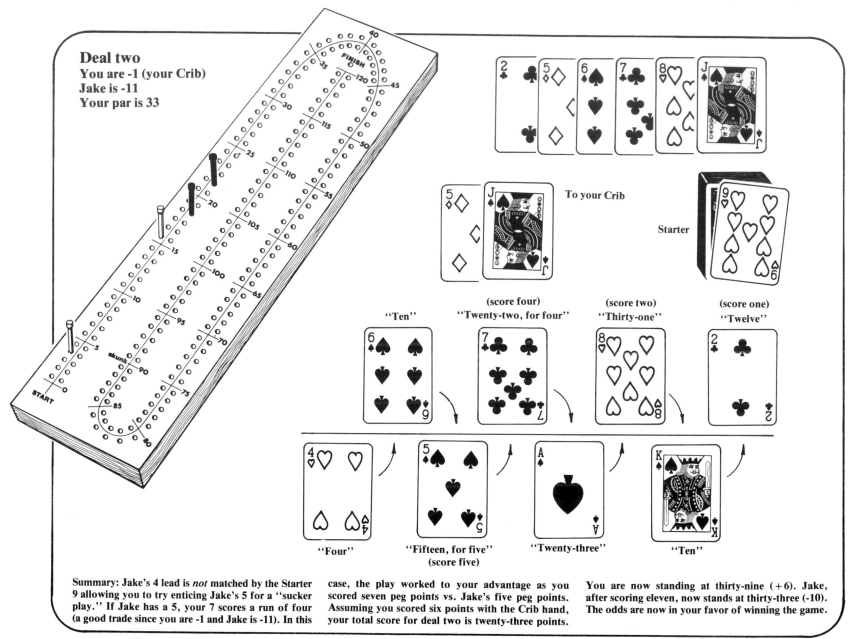

Deal two

You are -1 (your Crib)
Jake is -11
Your par is 33

To your Crib

Starter

"Ten"

(score four)
"Twenty-two, for four"

(score two)
"Thirty-one"

(score one)
"Twelve"

"Four"

"Fifteen, for five"
(score five)

"Twenty-three"

"Ten"

Summary: Jake's 4 lead is *not* matched by the Starter 9 allowing you to try enticing Jake's 5 for a "sucker play." If Jake has a 5, your 7 scores a run of four (a good trade since you are -1 and Jake is -11). In this case, the play worked to your advantage as you scored seven peg points vs. Jake's five peg points. Assuming you scored six points with the Crib hand, your total score for deal two is twenty-three points. You are now standing at thirty-nine (+6). Jake, after scoring eleven, now stands at thirty-three (-10). The odds are now in your favor of winning the game.

Deal two. Your score: 39 (+6). Jake's score: 33 (-10).

Deal three

You are +6
Jake is -10 and has the Crib
Your par is 43

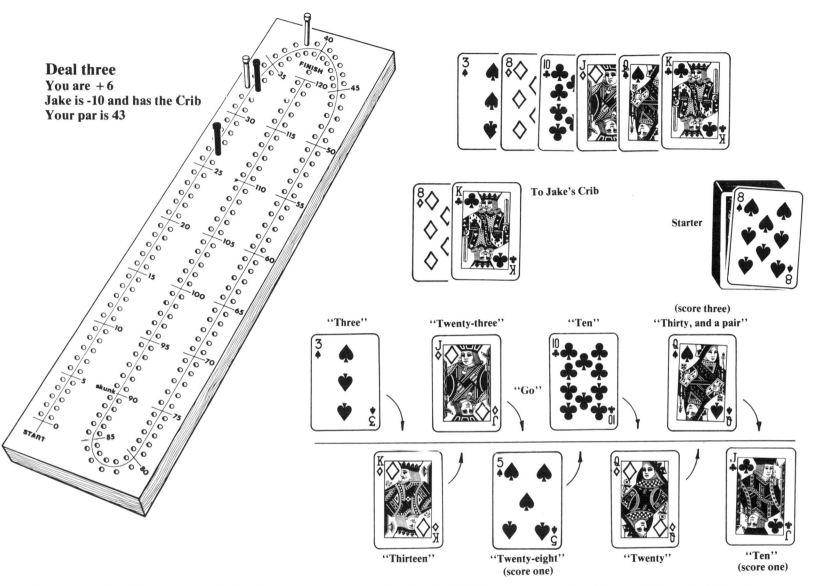

To Jake's Crib

Starter

(score three)

"Three"   "Twenty-three"   "Ten"   "Thirty, and a pair"

"Go"

"Thirteen"   "Twenty-eight"   "Twenty"   "Ten"
              (score one)   (score one)

Summary: keeping the 3 instead of the King is a "percentage" play. Leading a King has a 66% risk of being scored upon (no bias) vs. only a 28% risk (no bias) when a lone 3 is led. The 3 may be answered by a "ten" card that could be safely paired by you (in the example, alas, Jake played a King). Since you are +6, you "dump" the Jack as your second play. If you were minus to par, the Jack would be held for "desperation" offense, hoping to pair Jake's Jack later, if possible. Your total score for deal three is six points. You stand at forty-five (+2). Jake scored a six-point Crib and totaled seventeen points. Standing at fifty, Jake is now -9. Your advantage dwindled somewhat but you are still in the driver's seat. Your strategy is still offense (maximum).

Deal three. Your score: 45 (+2). Jake's score: 50 (-9).

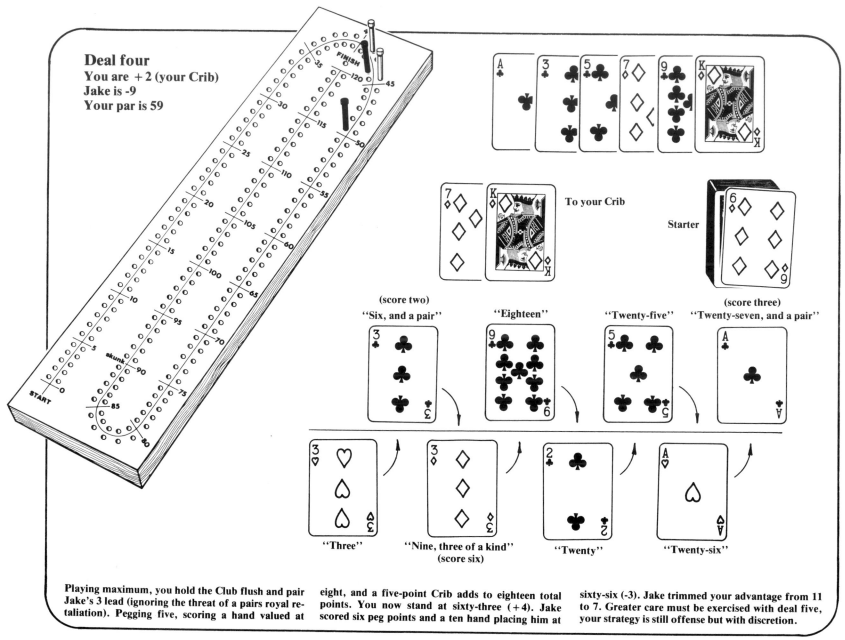

Deal four

You are + 2 (your Crib)

Jake is -9

Your par is 59

To your Crib

Starter

(score two)

"Six, and a pair"   "Eighteen"   "Twenty-five"   (score three)
"Twenty-seven, and a pair"

"Three"   "Nine, three of a kind"   "Twenty"   "Twenty-six"
(score six)

Playing maximum, you hold the Club flush and pair Jake's 3 lead (ignoring the threat of a pairs royal retaliation). Pegging five, scoring a hand valued at eight, and a five-point Crib adds to eighteen total points. You now stand at sixty-three (+4). Jake scored six peg points and a ten hand placing him at sixty-six (-3). Jake trimmed your advantage from 11 to 7. Greater care must be exercised with deal five, your strategy is still offense but with discretion.

Deal four. Your score: 63 (+4). Jake's score: 66 (-3).

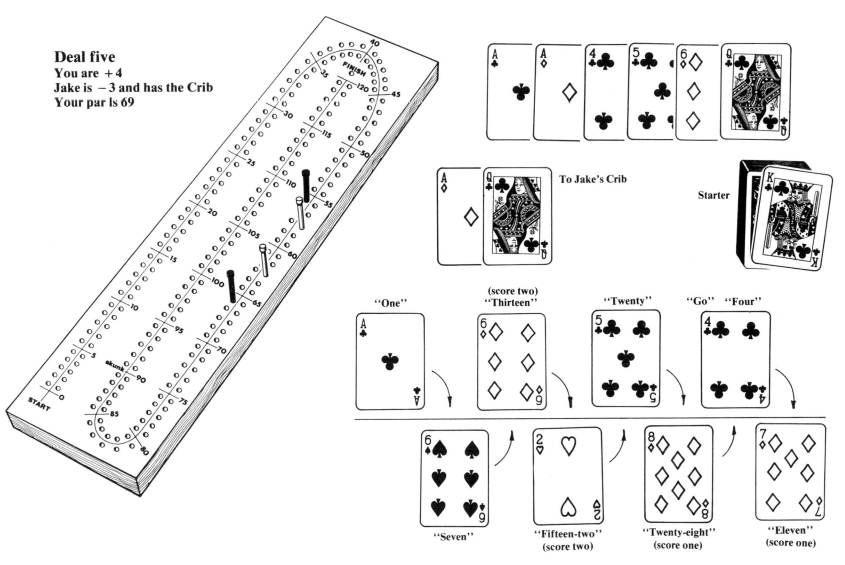

Deal five

You are +4
Jake is −3 and has the Crib
Your par Is 69

To Jake's Crib

Starter

"One"

(score two)
"Thirteen"

"Twenty"

"Go"   "Four"

"Seven"

"Fifteen-two"
(score two)

"Twenty-eight"
(score one)

"Eleven"
(score one)

Summary: playing maximum, your discard to Jake's Crib would be the pair of Aces. Caution must be exercised as Jake is only −3 of winning in *eight* deals. Keeping the Ace-4-5-6 for an almost sure seven point hand (only a 2 Starter "misses" this hand), maintaining par or better (sixty-nine). You lead the "safe" Ace. Jake's 6 response does *not* combine with the Starter King making your 6 pair a less risky play. If the Starter were a 5-6-7 or 9 you would be wise to "lay off" the pair as Jake may well have a "barnburner," picking up his −3 to par and winning in eight deals. You score eleven points and stand at seventy-four (+5). Jake scored a three-point Crib, four-peg points and a seven-point hand and stands at eighty (−5). Deal five strengthened your advantage. Your strategy remains the same: offense with discretion.

Deal five. Your score: 74 (+5). Jake's score: 80 (−5).

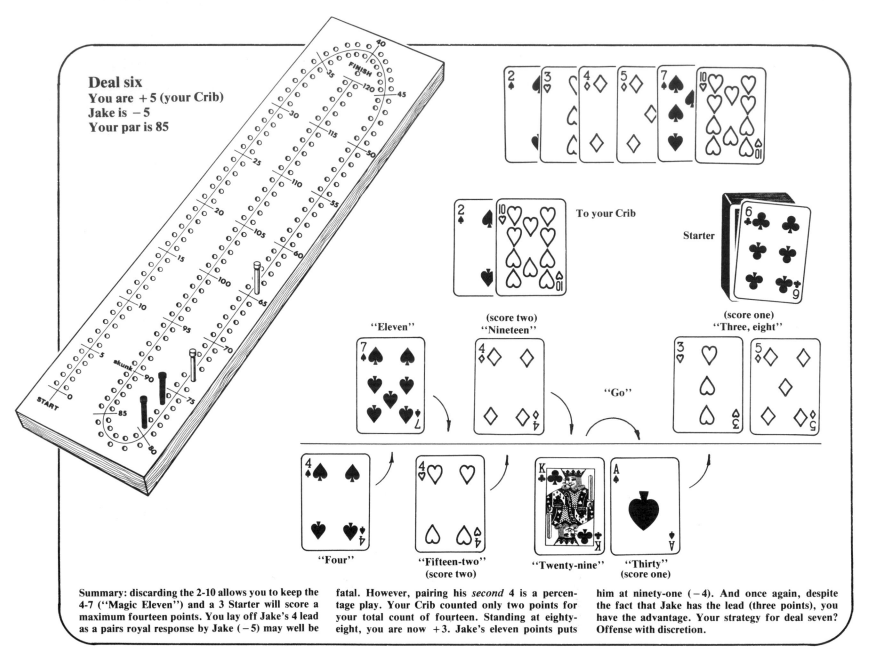

Deal six
You are +5 (your Crib)
Jake is −5
Your par is 85

To your Crib

Starter

(score two)
"Nineteen"

(score one)
"Three, eight"

"Eleven"

"Go"

"Four"

"Fifteen-two"
(score two)

"Twenty-nine"

"Thirty"
(score one)

Summary: discarding the 2-10 allows you to keep the 4-7 ("Magic Eleven") and a 3 Starter will score a maximum fourteen points. You lay off Jake's 4 lead as a pairs royal response by Jake (−5) may well be fatal. However, pairing his *second* 4 is a percentage play. Your Crib counted only two points for your total count of fourteen. Standing at eighty-eight, you are now +3. Jake's eleven points puts him at ninety-one (−4). And once again, despite the fact that Jake has the lead (three points), you have the advantage. Your strategy for deal seven? Offense with discretion.

Deal six. Your score: 88 (+3). Jake's score: 91 (−4).

Deal seven

You are +3
Jake is −4 and has the Crib
Your par is 95

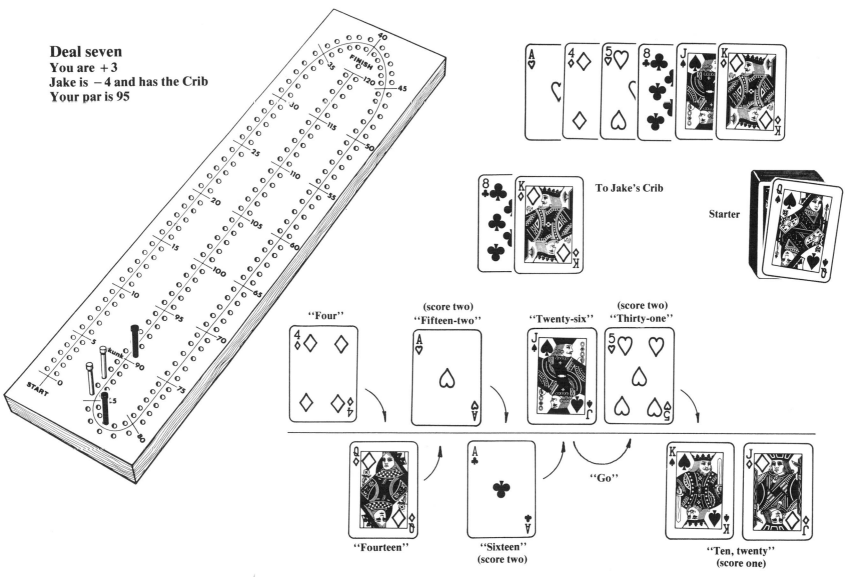

To Jake's Crib

Starter

"Four"

(score two)
"Fifteen-two"

"Twenty-six"

(score two)
"Thirty-one"

"Go"

"Fourteen"

"Sixteen"
(score two)

"Ten, twenty"
(score one)

Summary: you discard offensively, holding for maximum score. The Starter doubles your count and insures you of reaching at least "par" (ninety-five). Since par is assured, you lead *defensively* (Jake is only −4) with the 4. Your score for deal seven totals thirteen and you are standing at 101 (+6). Jake scored a six-point Crib for a total count of seventeen, and is now standing at 108 (−3). Deal eight must be played with extreme caution as Jake has about one chance in four of scoring thirteen points to win the game (and he has first count). Unless your eighth deal hand is a complete bust, defense is the byword.

Deal seven. Your score: 101 (+6). Jake's score: 108 (−3).

97

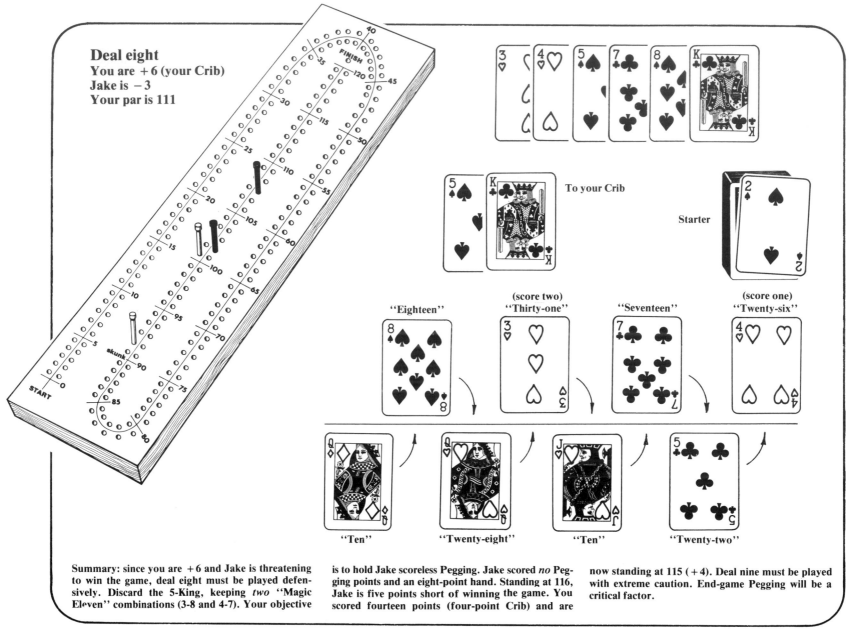

Deal eight

You are +6 (your Crib)
Jake is −3
Your par is 111

To your Crib

Starter

| "Eighteen" | (score two) "Thirty-one" | "Seventeen" | (score one) "Twenty-six" |

| "Ten" | "Twenty-eight" | "Ten" | "Twenty-two" |

Summary: since you are +6 and Jake is threatening to win the game, deal eight must be played defensively. Discard the 5-King, keeping *two* "Magic Eleven" combinations (3-8 and 4-7). Your objective is to hold Jake scoreless Pegging. Jake scored *no* Pegging points and an eight-point hand. Standing at 116, Jake is five points short of winning the game. You scored fourteen points (four-point Crib) and are now standing at 115 (+4). Deal nine must be played with extreme caution. End-game Pegging will be a critical factor.

Deal eight. Your score: 115 (+4). Jake's score: 116 (−5).

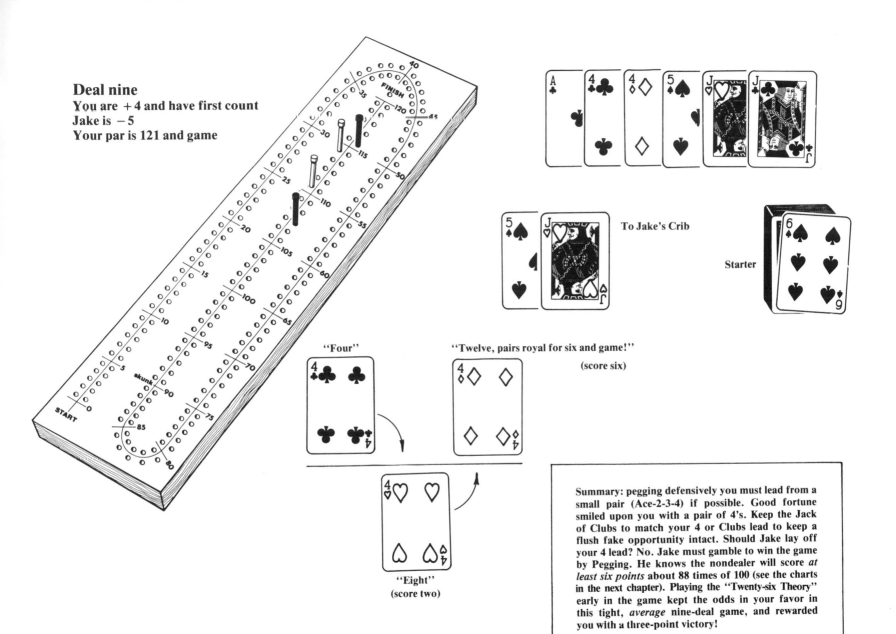

Deal nine
You are +4 and have first count
Jake is −5
Your par is 121 and game

To Jake's Crib

Starter

"Four"

"Twelve, pairs royal for six and game!"

(score six)

"Eight"
(score two)

Summary: pegging defensively you must lead from a small pair (Ace-2-3-4) if possible. Good fortune smiled upon you with a pair of 4's. Keep the Jack of Clubs to match your 4 or Clubs lead to keep a flush fake opportunity intact. Should Jake lay off your 4 lead? No. Jake must gamble to win the game by Pegging. He knows the nondealer will score *at least six points* about 88 times of 100 (see the charts in the next chapter). Playing the "Twenty-six Theory" early in the game kept the odds in your favor in this tight, *average* nine-deal game, and rewarded you with a three-point victory!

Let's review the game we've just played. Manipulating a game of Cribbage on paper as we have just done to come up with a desired result is, of course, easy. However, about four games in ten *will* be played somewhat like the game illustrated. The game was decided on the ninth deal by "end-game" Pegging. And by playing the "Twenty-six Theory," the non-dealer of the first hand won the game. In this near-average game, many players—even very good players—would have *lost* by playing conservatively early in the game. For example, risking a high-counting Crib for Jake in deal one (King-Queen discard) in order to "cover" your 3 lead with a 9 was rewarded with two peg points. The "sucker" play in deal two (4-6-5-7), resulting in seven peg points, was the key play of the game, helping you attain a +6 at that point. Despite being behind after playing hand three (50-45) the odds remained in your favor throughout the remainder of the game. Playing the "Twenty-six Theory" *the non-dealer was in range of winning the game with first count on the ninth deal.*

Now, let's go through a few typical game situations played by the dealer of the first hand. Since the first dealer is plus-nine before the first card is played, and will count first on the tenth hand, defense is the byword. Your objective is to keep that plus-nine on the plus side of the ledger and Uncle Jake on the minus side of the ledger (Jake starts at minus-seven, of course).

Your game must be geared to board position at all times. . .playing the averages. There will be times when you and Uncle Jake are both near zero to the "par" holes. Your strategy then is governed by your hand, the Starter card, and whether Jake's first, or second, card match the Starter card (a potential "barnburner"). Early in the game, the general rule is play offense if there is doubt about whether to play offense or defense (both players are close to "par"). This general rule is valid for both dealer and the nondealer. However, in the later stages of the game, the general rule is to play defense. But again, check Jake's lead, the Starter card, and your hand. Consider the discard to the Crib, especially in relation to the Starter card. And does Jake's first lead minimize the Crib being a "barnburner" (if it's Jake's Crib)? You must thoroughly consider the Crib possibilities before committing yourself to offense or defense in the later stages of a tight game (and it's a good practice early in the game, too).

The reason for the shift in strategy in the later stages of the game is that it is easier to slow the game down than it is to speed it up. If you gamble offensively early in the game and fail, there will be ample time to work on your defense and still win the game. However, if you gamble offensively in the later stages of the game, and fail, you will have lost control of the game.

Once again, study the odds in the next chapter pertaining to average points scored per hand (the nondealer's) and average points scored by the dealer (including the Crib). These odds will give you the necessary insight on when to gamble and play offensively, and when to play defensively. And remember, hunch players are losers! Play the odds!

Let's review a few hands, analyzing the strategy of the dealer of the first hand. . .playing the "Twenty-six Theory":

Playing the "Twenty-six Theory"

Deal One. As the dealer you are +9.
Your par is 7.

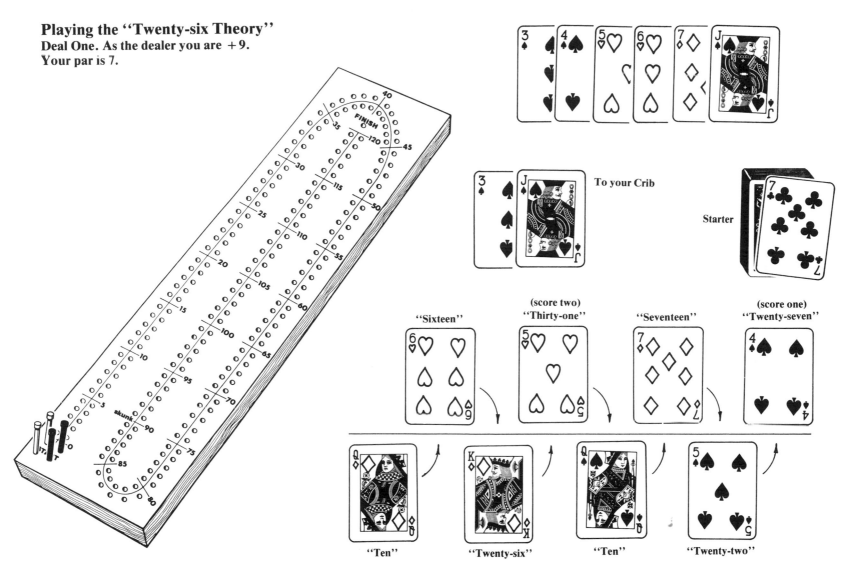

To your Crib

Starter

"Sixteen"	(score two) "Thirty-one"	"Seventeen"	(score one) "Twenty-seven"

"Ten"	"Twenty-six"	"Ten"	"Twenty-two"

Summary: as the dealer your goal is to hold the nondealer scoreless Pegging. Do *not* destroy your hand in discarding to your Crib, however, in an attempt to keep defensive Pegging cards. But peg defensively! Hold Jake scoreless if at all possible. In the hand illustrated, playing a 6 on Jake's Queen lead holds Jake scoreless. You have sacrificed two points in the process, but the defensive trade is to the dealer's advantage (+9). Remember, Jake, as the nondealer is −7 to par. You succeed in holding Jake scoreless Pegging. Jake's score: eight points (−9). Your Crib contained six points and after deal one you stand at twenty-one (+14).

Deal one. Your score: 21 (+14). Jake's score: 8 (−9).

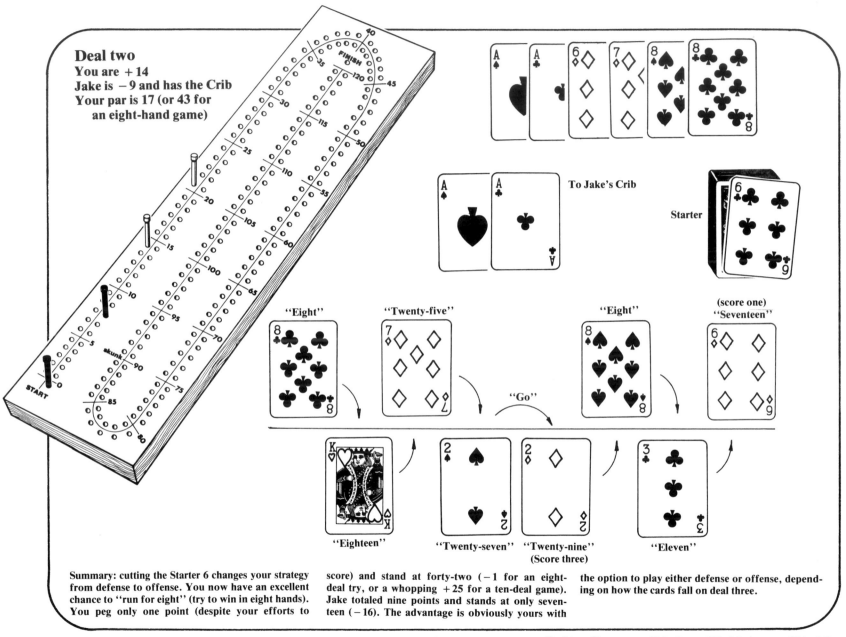

Deal two
You are +14
Jake is −9 and has the Crib
Your par is 17 (or 43 for
    an eight-hand game)

To Jake's Crib

Starter

"Eight"   "Twenty-five"   "Eight"   (score one) "Seventeen"

"Go"

"Eighteen"   "Twenty-seven"   "Twenty-nine"   "Eleven"
                             (Score three)

Summary: cutting the Starter 6 changes your strategy from defense to offense. You now have an excellent chance to "run for eight" (try to win in eight hands). You peg only one point (despite your efforts to score) and stand at forty-two (−1 for an eight-deal try, or a whopping +25 for a ten-deal game). Jake totaled nine points and stands at only seventeen (−16). The advantage is obviously yours with the option to play either defense or offense, depending on how the cards fall on deal three.

Deal two. Your score: 42 (−1 or +25). Jake's score: 17 (−16).

Deal three

You are −1 or +25 (your Crib)
Jake is −16
Your par is 59 (eight deal try)

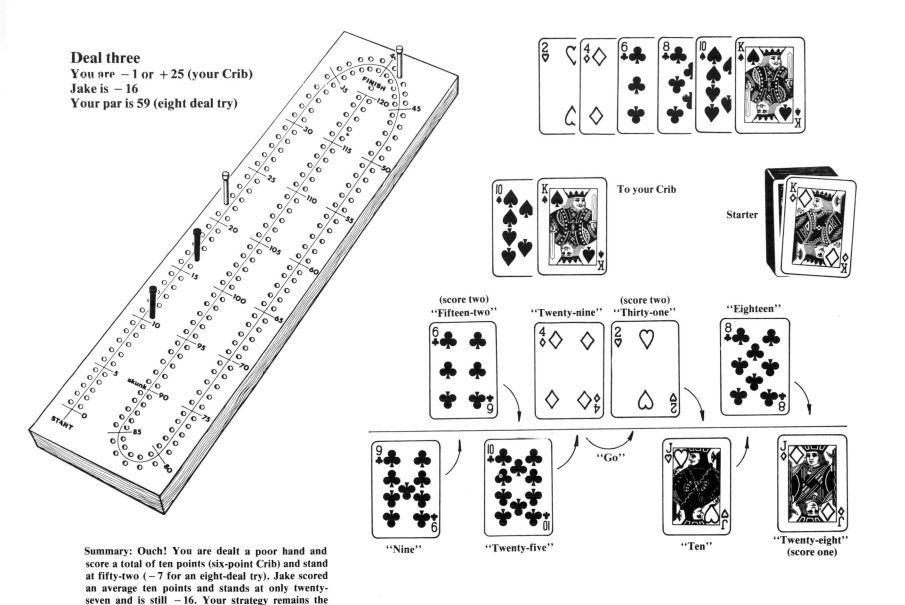

To your Crib

Starter

(score two)
"Fifteen-two" "Twenty-nine" (score two)
"Thirty-one" "Eighteen"

"Nine" "Twenty-five" "Go" "Ten" "Twenty-eight"
(score one)

Summary: Ouch! You are dealt a poor hand and score a total of ten points (six-point Crib) and stand at fifty-two (−7 for an eight-deal try). Jake scored an average ten points and stands at only twenty-seven and is still −16. Your strategy remains the same. You have the option of playing offensively or defensively on deal four.

Deal three. Your score: 52 (−7 or +19). Jake's score: 27 (−16).

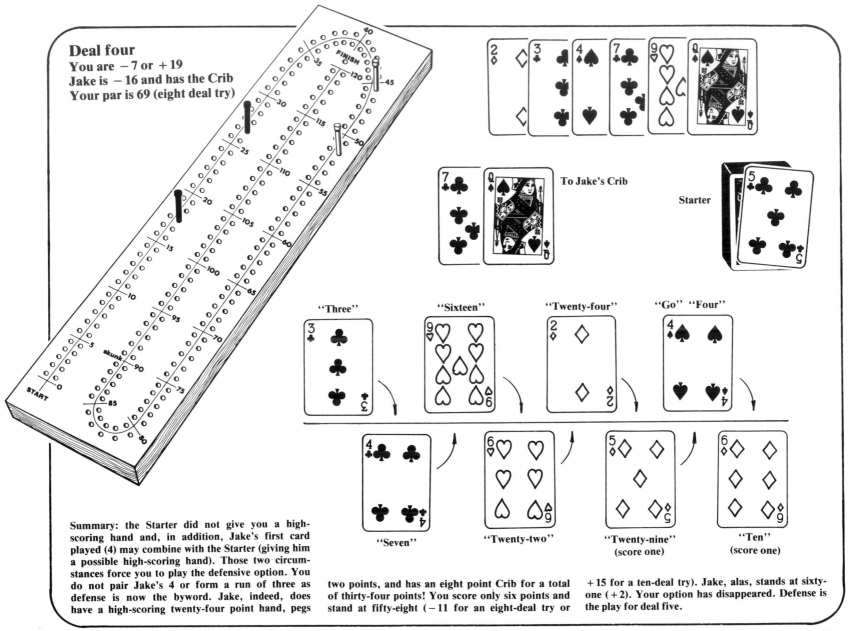

Deal four

You are −7 or +19
Jake is −16 and has the Crib
Your par is 69 (eight deal try)

To Jake's Crib

Starter

"Three"   "Sixteen"   "Twenty-four"   "Go" "Four"

"Seven"   "Twenty-two"   "Twenty-nine"   "Ten"
                          (score one)   (score one)

Summary: the Starter did not give you a high-scoring hand and, in addition, Jake's first card played (4) may combine with the Starter (giving him a possible high-scoring hand). Those two circumstances force you to play the defensive option. You do not pair Jake's 4 or form a run of three as defense is now the byword. Jake, indeed, does have a high-scoring twenty-four point hand, pegs two points, and has an eight point Crib for a total of thirty-four points! You score only six points and stand at fifty-eight (−11 for an eight-deal try or +15 for a ten-deal try). Jake, alas, stands at sixty-one (+2). Your option has disappeared. Defense is the play for deal five.

Deal four. Your score: 58 (−11 or +15). Jake's score: 61 (+2).

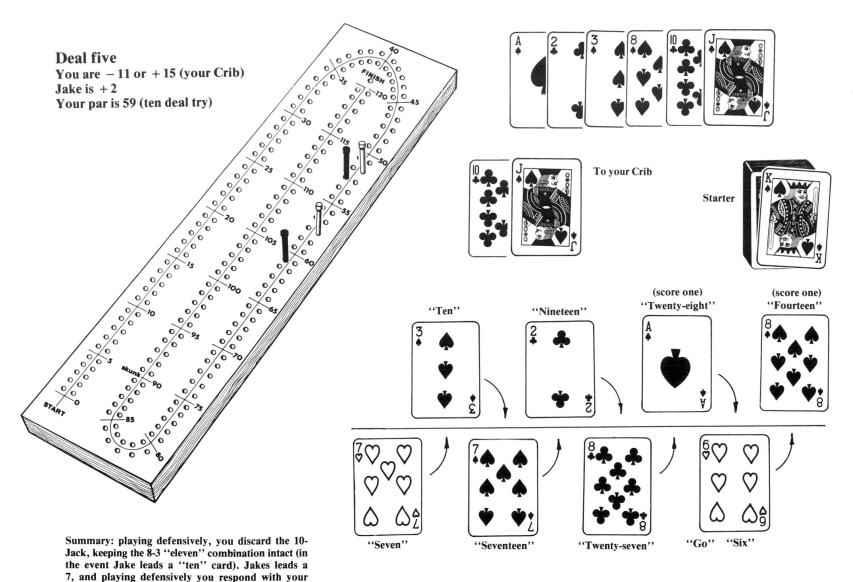

Deal five
You are − 11 or + 15 (your Crib)
Jake is + 2
Your par is 59 (ten deal try)

To your Crib

Starter

(score one) | (score one)
"Ten" | "Nineteen" | "Twenty-eight" | "Fourteen"

"Seven" | "Seventeen" | "Twenty-seven" | "Go" "Six"

Summary: playing defensively, you discard the 10-Jack, keeping the 8-3 "eleven" combination intact (in the event Jake leads a "ten" card). Jakes leads a 7, and playing defensively you respond with your safest card (your 3). You continue to peg defensively and fortunately Jake fails to score. Unfortunately, Jake has a twelve-point hand and now stands at seventy-three (+4). You score four points in your Crib and now stand at 69 (+10). Trying for an eight-deal game at this point would be foolish.

Deal five. Your score: 69 (+ 10). Jake's score: 73 (+ 4).

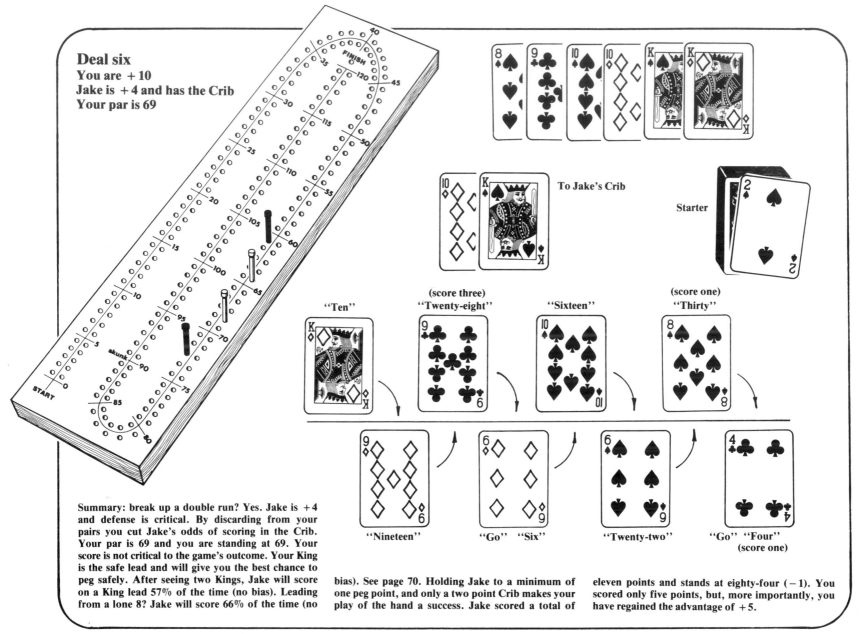

Deal six

You are +10

Jake is +4 and has the Crib

Your par is 69

To Jake's Crib

Starter

"Ten"   (score three) "Twenty-eight"   "Sixteen"   (score one) "Thirty"

"Nineteen"   "Go" "Six"   "Twenty-two"   "Go" "Four" (score one)

Summary: break up a double run? Yes. Jake is +4 and defense is critical. By discarding from your pairs you cut Jake's odds of scoring in the Crib. Your par is 69 and you are standing at 69. Your score is not critical to the game's outcome. Your King is the safe lead and will give you the best chance to peg safely. After seeing two Kings, Jake will score on a King lead 57% of the time (no bias). Leading from a lone 8? Jake will score 66% of the time (no bias). See page 70. Holding Jake to a minimum of one peg point, and only a two point Crib makes your play of the hand a success. Jake scored a total of eleven points and stands at eighty-four (−1). You scored only five points, but, more importantly, you have regained the advantage of +5.

Deal six. Your score: 74 (+5). Jake's score: 84 (−1).

Deal seven
You are +5 (your Crib)
Jake ls −1
Your par is 85

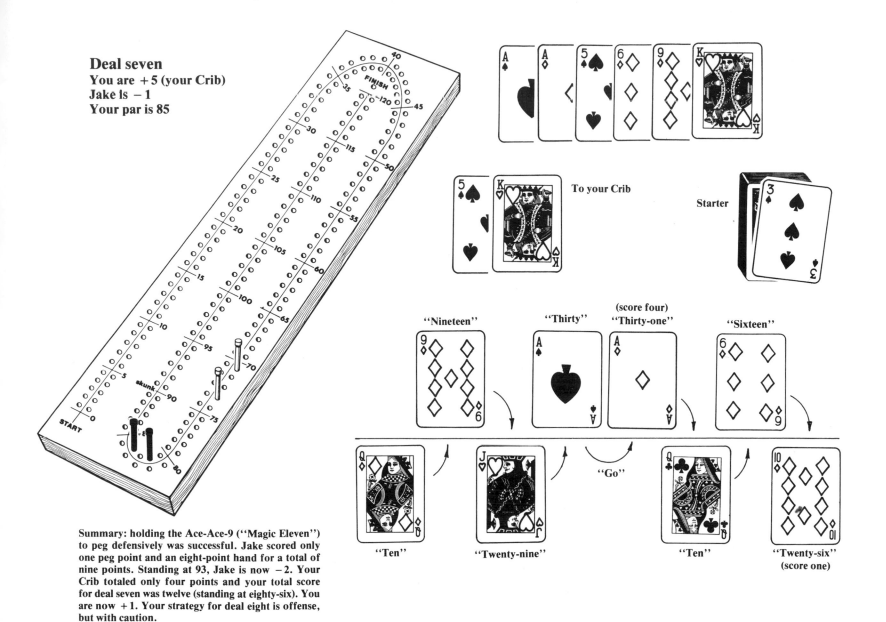

To your Crib

Starter

"Nineteen"　　　"Thirty"　　(score four) "Thirty-one"　　"Sixteen"

"Go"

"Ten"　　"Twenty-nine"　　"Ten"　　"Twenty-six" (score one)

Summary: holding the Ace-Ace-9 ("Magic Eleven") to peg defensively was successful. Jake scored only one peg point and an eight-point hand for a total of nine points. Standing at 93, Jake is now −2. Your Crib totaled only four points and your total score for deal seven was twelve (standing at eighty-six). You are now +1. Your strategy for deal eight is offense, but with caution.

Deal seven. Your score: 86 (+1). Jake's score: 93 (−2).

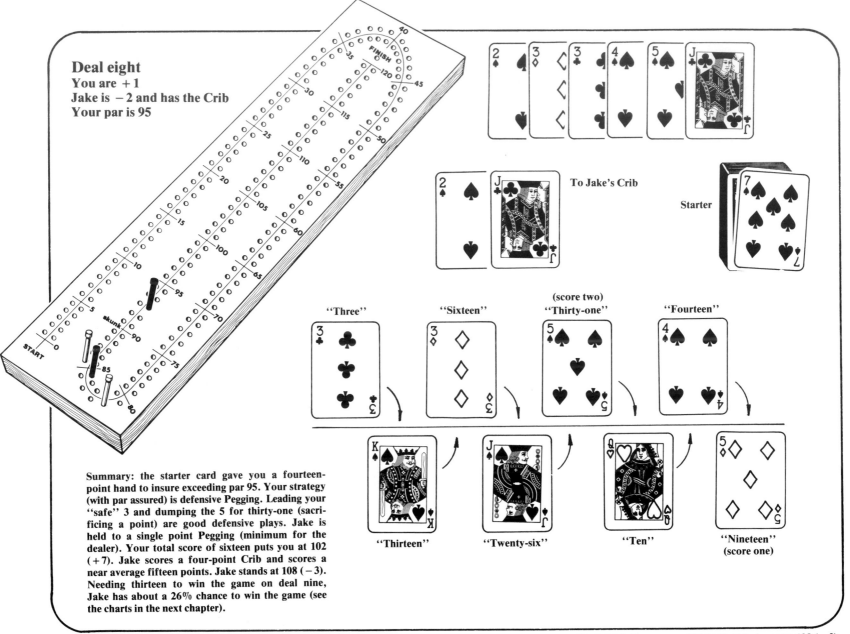

Deal eight
You are +1
Jake is −2 and has the Crib
Your par is 95

To Jake's Crib

Starter

"Three"   "Sixteen"   (score two) "Thirty-one"   "Fourteen"

"Thirteen"   "Twenty-six"   "Ten"   "Nineteen" (score one)

Summary: the starter card gave you a fourteen-point hand to insure exceeding par 95. Your strategy (with par assured) is defensive Pegging. Leading your "safe" 3 and dumping the 5 for thirty-one (sacrificing a point) are good defensive plays. Jake is held to a single point Pegging (minimum for the dealer). Your total score of sixteen puts you at 102 (+7). Jake scores a four-point Crib and scores a near average fifteen points. Jake stands at 108 (−3). Needing thirteen to win the game on deal nine, Jake has about a 26% chance to win the game (see the charts in the next chapter).

Deal eight. Your score: 102 (+7). Jake's score: 108 (−3).

Deal nine

You are | 7 (your Crib)
Jake is −3
Your par is 111

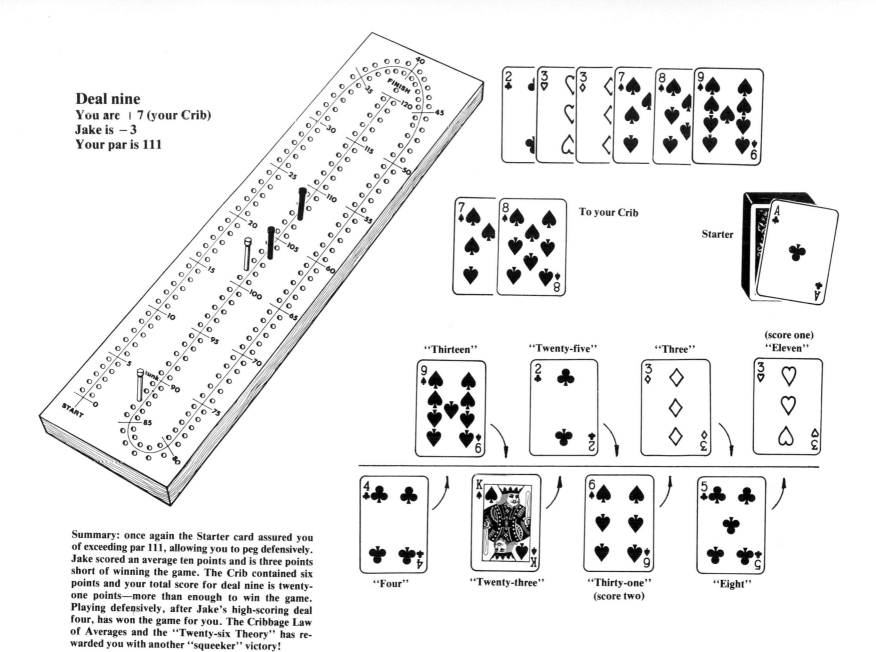

To your Crib

Starter

(score one)
"Eleven"

"Thirteen"   "Twenty-five"   "Three"

"Four"   "Twenty-three"   "Thirty-one"
(score two)   "Eight"

Summary: once again the Starter card assured you of exceeding par 111, allowing you to peg defensively. Jake scored an average ten points and is three points short of winning the game. The Crib contained six points and your total score for deal nine is twenty-one points—more than enough to win the game. Playing defensively, after Jake's high-scoring deal four, has won the game for you. The Cribbage Law of Averages and the "Twenty-six Theory" has rewarded you with another "squeeker" victory!

Reviewing the game, we find how a high-scoring hand by either player can change strategy from defense to offense and back again. Your high-scoring second hand (twenty-one points nondealing) gave you the option of offensive or defensive play. Jake's twenty-four point fourth deal hand regained the advantage and your play was defensive for the remainder of the game. And despite Jake scoring average, or near average hands from that point on, your defensive Pegging strategy (a decision based on the "Twenty-six Theory's" par points) rewarded you with a narrow victory.

Of course, the game was manipulated, with a favorable outcome. Many games will not be played as closely to average as the game illustrated. Time and time again your strategy will backfire. But hang in there. That old Cribbage Law of Averages and the "Twenty-six Theory" will pay off! It should reward you with an increase of about 6% in your winning edge. And playing opponents like Jake the Snake, that's the winning edge!

Now you have the complete game! The only missing ingredient is your analysis of *your own game*. Begin an analysis of *all* your games, with *all* your opponents. Keep running averages of games, points scored per hand, your winning percentage against each player, and your average point margin of victory (or, heaven forbid, your average point margin of losing). Work to improve your averages. Analyze your game thoroughly. You'll be amazed how these "dry" statistics will begin to pay off for you. You may discover that your averages are slightly different from the "Twenty-six Theory." In fact, Cribbage experts differ on their opinion of the averages. They range from "Twenty-five" up to "Twenty-nine" for a two-hand average. Keep your own scores. If your average differs widely, you may want to play your own theory.

But, whatever you do, make Lord Kelvin proud of you. Keep a book on all your opponents. In the back of this book are some score sheets to aid you in your bookkeeping. A quick, easy way to keep a running record is to mark your winning games with the score, or number of points you won by (Jake is beaten, and ends in the 101st hole—mark "20" in your book), and mark your losses with the number of points you lose by—and circle that number. . .a very quick, simple process. Get in the habit of playing with your book, and in your leisure time, analyze the results.

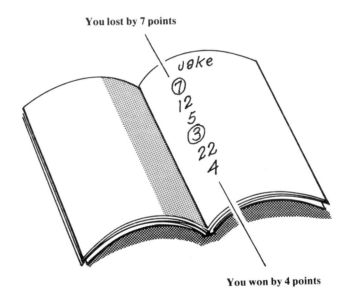

You lost by 7 points

You won by 4 points

The next chapter will give you some insights as to the odds of scoring in Cribbage, and what your winning—or losing—averages mean in terms of what you can expect to win—or lose—in this frustratingly simple game of Cribbage! This fascinating, exciting game of Cribbage!

What's the Odds?

What's the Odds?

Many games of Cribbage are won or lost by simply *knowing the odds* and playing your hand accordingly. Study the next few pages and you will improve your knowledge of Cribbage probabilities. These probability tidbits are especially helpful when playing those last crucial hands. . .and that crucial "end-game Pegging" that decides so many games.

Remember, hunch players are losers. Play the odds, and sooner or later you will be rewarded with victories.

The charts are based on samples of 1,000. Your own games should parallel these findings. Of course, millions of games would have to be analyzed to pinpoint these probablities precisely. And this is what makes Cribbage such an exciting game. . .the endless combinations of cards and Pegging possibilities.

The chart to the right analyzes the number of deals in a typical Cribbage game, and who has the advantage (the dealer or the nondealer). The chart shows that a nine-deal game is by far the most common (about 42% of all games are played in nine deals). The lower chart shows that the dealer wins about 19% more than the nondealer (250-170) in a nine-deal game. It also shows that about 90% of all games are played in eight, nine, or ten deals. But the ninth deal is the critical deal. In an *average* game, the nondealer comes up about five points short, and the dealer wins—usually by counting his Crib to win the game. By using the "Twenty-six Theory" as your guide, you can *cut* the dealer's ninth deal advantage.

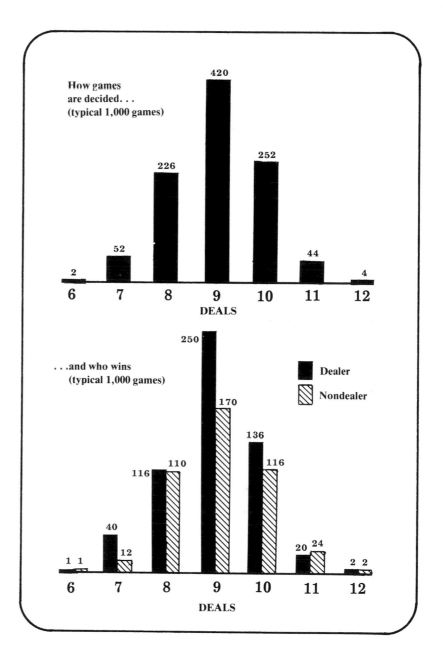

Nondealer Hand Analysis
(including Pegging)
Typical 1,000 hands

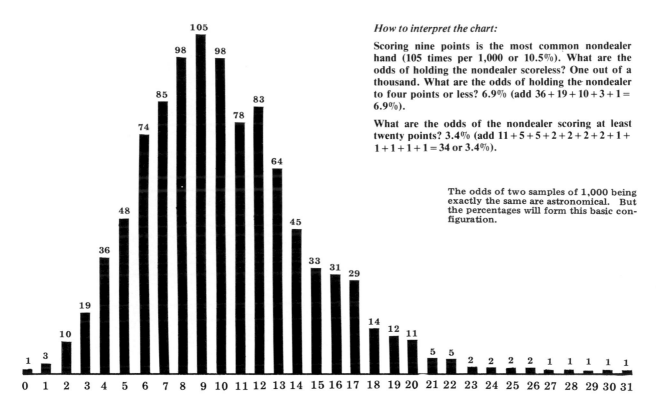

How to interpret the chart:

Scoring nine points is the most common nondealer hand (105 times per 1,000 or 10.5%). What are the odds of holding the nondealer scoreless? One out of a thousand. What are the odds of holding the nondealer to four points or less? 6.9% (add $36 + 19 + 10 + 3 + 1 = 6.9\%$).

What are the odds of the nondealer scoring at least twenty points? 3.4% (add $11 + 5 + 5 + 2 + 2 + 2 + 2 + 1 + 1 + 1 + 1 + 1 = 34$ or 3.4%).

The odds of two samples of 1,000 being exactly the same are astronomical. But the percentages will form this basic configuration.

TOTAL POINTS SCORED (including Pegging)

Dealer Hand Analysis
(including Pegging and Crib)
Typical 1,000 hands

The odds of two samples of 1,000 being exactly the same are astronomical. But the percentages will form this basic configuration.

How to interpret the chart:

Can the dealer be held scoreless? No. the dealer *always* pegs at least one point. The odds of holding the dealer to one point? One out of a thousand. And the odds of scoring forty or more points? 500 to 1 (1 + 1 = 2 of 1,000). The most common hand for the dealer? Fifteen (87 of 1,000).

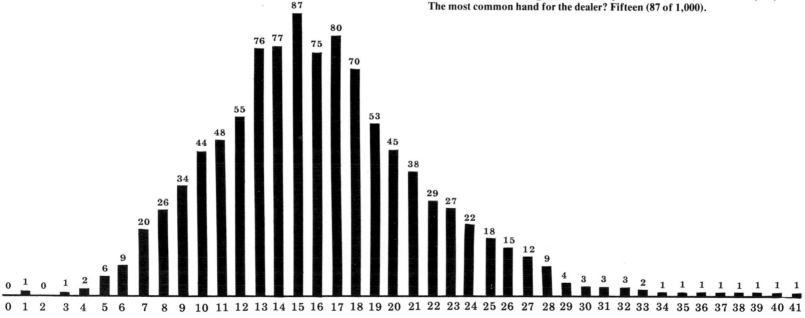

TOTAL POINTS SCORED (including Pegging and Crib)

*What's the odds of holding the nondealer:			*What's the odds of the nondealer scoring:			**What's the odds of holding the dealer:			**What's the odds of the dealer scoring:	
Points	*Odds*		*Points* (or more)	*Odds*		*Points*	*Odds*		*Points* (or more)	*Odds*
0	1,000 to 1		31	1,000 to 1		0	Not Possible		41	1,000 to 1
1	250 to 1		30	500 to 1		1	1,000 to 1		40	500 to 1
2	70 to 1		29	333 to 1		2	1,000 to 1		39	333 to 1
3	33 to 1		28	250 to 1		3	500 to 1		38	250 to 1
4	14 to 1		27	200 to 1		4	250 to 1		37	200 to 1
5	8½ to 1		26	143 to 1		5	100 to 1		36	167 to 1
6	5 to 1		25	111 to 1		6	53 to 1		35	143 to 1
7	4 to 1		24	91 to 1		7	21 to 1		34	125 to 1
8	2½ to 1		23	77 to 1		8	13 to 1		33	100 to 1
9	Even		22	56 to 1		9	9 to 1		32	77 to 1
			21	44 to 1		10	6½ to 1		31	63 to 1
			20	29 to 1		11	5 to 1		30	53 to 1
			19	22 to 1		12	4 to 1		29	43 to 1
			18	17 to 1		13	3 to 1		28	31 to 1
			17	11 to 1		14	2½ to 1		27	23 to 1
			16	8 to 1		15	Even		26	17 to 1
			15	7 to 1					25	13 to 1
			14	5 to 1					24	10 to 1
			13	4 to 1					23	8 to 1
			12	3 to 1					22	6½ to 1
			11	2½ to 1					21	5 to 1
			10	Even					20	4 to 1
									19	3½ to 1
									18	3 to 1
									17	2 to 1
									16	Even

*Including Pegging

**Including Pegging and the Crib

Nondealer Hand Analysis
Typical 1,000 hands

Average: 8.1 per hand

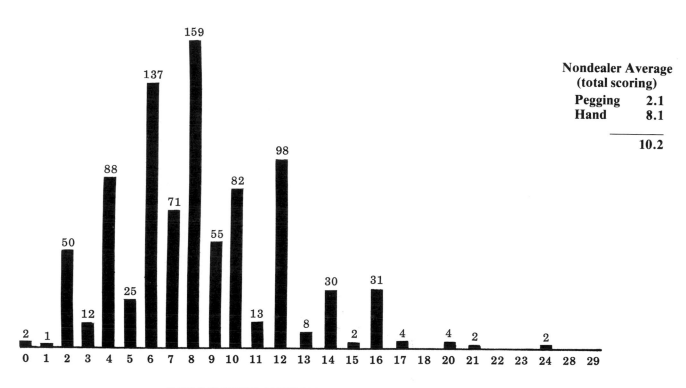

POINTS SCORED BY NONDEALER'S HAND

**Nondealer Average
(total scoring)**

Pegging	2.1
Hand	8.1
	10.2

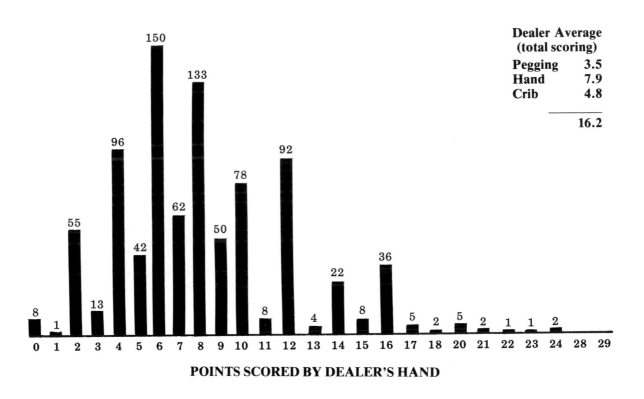

Dealer Hand Analysis
Typical 1,000 hands

Average: 7.9 per hand

POINTS SCORED BY DEALER'S HAND

Dealer Average (total scoring)	
Pegging	3.5
Hand	7.9
Crib	4.8
	16.2

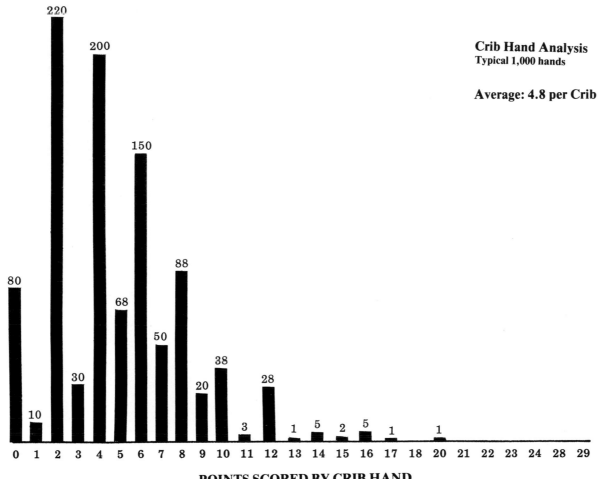

Crib Hand Analysis
Typical 1,000 hands

Average: 4.8 per Crib

POINTS SCORED BY CRIB HAND

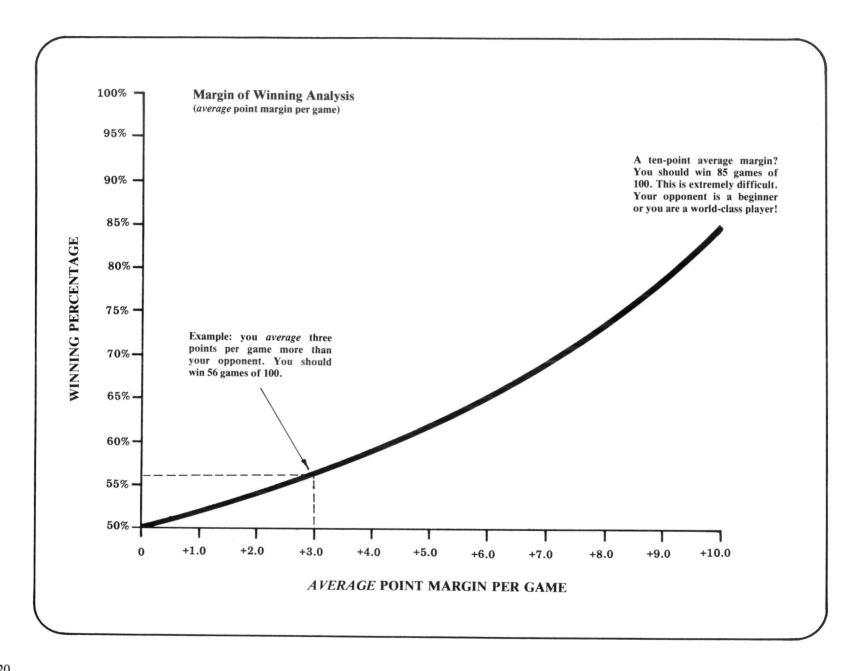

Margin of Winning Analysis
(*average* point margin per game)

A ten-point average margin? You should win **85** games of 100. This is extremely difficult. Your opponent is a beginner or you are a world-class player!

Example: you *average* three points per game more than your opponent. You should win 56 games of 100.

WINNING PERCENTAGE

AVERAGE POINT MARGIN PER GAME

29 Hand: 500,000 to 1
(approximate)

28 Hand: 50,000 to 1
(approximate)

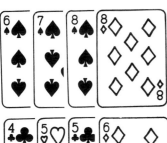 

24 Hand: 200 to 1
(approximate)

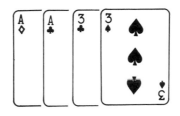

*Drawing a 2?
(inside quadruple run)

11.5 to 1

*Drawing a 9 or Queen?
(both ends open quadruple run)

5.75 to 1

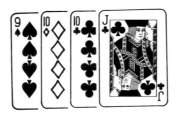

*Drawing a 9, 10 or Jack?
(doubling a double run)

5.75 to 1

*Drawing a 5, Jack, Queen or King?
(doubling a 5-''ten-card'' run combination)

3.8 to 1

*Provided you have *not* discarded a helping card

121

Appendix

Five-Card Cribbage
(Sir John Suckling's original game)

Sir John's game was played with only five cards dealt to each player instead of the modern game's six-card deal.

The game is usually played to sixty-one, with a lurch, or skunk, attained if a player fails to score at least thirty-one. The game may also be played to 121 points (with a lurch attained if a player fails to score ninety-one).

To begin play, each player cuts the deck. The player cutting the high card is the first hand's dealer. The nondealer is entitled to immediately score three points to compensate for the advantage the deal gives the dealer. A peculiarity in the rules allows the nondealer to score these three points at any time during the game if he so chooses (except *after* his opponent has scored the winning point).

The dealer then deals five cards to his opponent and five to himself, alternating between the two and dealing one card at a time.

Each player discards two cards to form the dealer's Crib. The nondealer discards first.

The nondealer then cuts the deck, and the dealer turns up the top card of the cut deck. This is the Starter card and it scores the same as in six-card Cribbage.

Pegging then begins with the nondealer playing the first card. Pegging is scored in the same manner as six-card Cribbage, *except* play stops at the first "Go" or the first "thirty-one." If a player scores exactly "thirty-one" he scores two points. If play stops at a "Go," the player playing the last card scores one point.

The Crib has more importance in five-card Cribbage than in the six-card variation. The Crib contains five cards (including the Starter) while the hand contains only four cards (including the Starter).

Flushes are scored as in six-card Cribbage. The hand may score a three-card flush (all the cards in the hand are the same suit) or a four-card flush (the Starter is also of the same suit). The Crib, however, must have all five cards of the same suit to score the flush bonus (five points).

Since the hand consists of only four cards, instead of five in six-card Cribbage, scoring is somewhat lower. Pegging to "thirty-one" only once keeps this aspect of scoring lower also. The averages every two deals are about ten points less than the six-card game (sixteen vs. twenty-six points).

And despite Edmond Hoyle's criticism of six-card Cribbage, the five-card variation eliminates much of the fun of Pegging. The traps, the flush fakes, and, in general, much of the Pegging strategy is simply not used when Pegging up to "thirty-one" only once.

Three-hand Cribbage

The rules of Three-hand Cribbage are similar to Two-hand six-card Cribbage.

Many Cribbage boards have a third track to accommodate this game, but if your board has only two tracks, you may improvise by moving pegs side to side or track to track to avoid scoring conflicts. Each player has two pegs, preferably of different colors.

The game usually consists of sixty-one points, but players may agree to play to 121.

The three players cut the deck. The player cutting the low card deals first. The deal then rotates clockwise.

The dealer deals five cards to each player in a clockwise rotation, one at a time. After the fifteen cards are dealt, the dealer deals a sixteenth card to himself. This card is the foundation of the Crib. All players then discard one card from their hand to form the Crib.

The player to the left of the dealer cuts the Starter card. This player also begins Pegging.

After Pegging, the hands and Crib are scored. The player to the left of the dealer scores first. The dealer scores his hand and Crib last.

All three players are independent, and strategy usually involves two players balking the leader and trying to improve their positions.

The winner, of course, scores double—one from each of his opponents. A player will be even if he wins one of three games.

Hands and Cribs will score about the same as Two-hand six-card Cribbage. Since you discard only one card to your own Crib, it is somewhat more difficult to "salt." Sir Edmond Hoyle was somewhat critical of the game, saying, "ordinarily it is a poor-enough affair."

Four-hand Cribbage

In general, the rules for Four-hand Cribbage are the same as for Two-hand six-card Cribbage. The game may be sixty-one or 121 points.

Play is by partnership. Partners are determined by cutting the deck, with the two players cutting low being paired against the two players cutting high. Of course, partners may be teamed by mutual agreement.

Partners sit opposite each other. One player from each partnership is chosen to peg the score. Although his partner cannot touch the page, he should carefully check for accuracy in Pegging. Partners should also check each other's scoring of hands and Crib to insure accuracy.

One player from each partnership cuts for the deal. The low cut wins the first deal.

The dealer shuffles the pack and the player *to the right* of the dealer cuts the deck (an unusual Cribbage rule). The dealer then deals one card at a time, beginning with the player *to his left*, until all players have five cards.

Each player discards one card to the dealer to form the Crib. Of course, you discard cards to form a strong Crib if it is your Crib or your partner's Crib, and discard balking cards to your opponent's Crib.

The player *to the dealer's left* then cuts the deck and the dealer turns up the Starter card in the same manner as in Two-hand six-card Cribbage.

The player to the dealer's left plays the first card. Pegging is scored in the same manner as for Two-hand six-card Cribbage. Extra care must be taken in scoring as sixteen cards are played and scored instead of eight. Care must be taken to insure that a "Go" is completely played out. For example, a player plays a 2 for "twenty-nine," and the other three players announce "Go." The player playing the first 2 then may play a second 2 for "thirty-one" and score four points.

After Pegging, the player to the dealer's left scores his hand and scoring continues clockwise around the table. The dealer counts his hand and Crib last.

Pegging assumes more importance than in Two-hand Cribbage, as twice as many cards are counted, scoring more points as a consequence.

Scoring an extra hand and with the additional peg points, the averages every two deals are about forty-three points vs. twenty-six for the two-hand six-card game.

Six-hand Cribbage

A variation of the four-hand game is played with three sets of partners. The rules and procedures are the same as for Four-hand Cribbage with the exception of dealing and seating.

Partners sit apart, separated by opposing players on the left and right.

The dealer deals five cards to four players and *only four cards* to the player to his right and to himself. The four players to his left discard one card to form his Crib.

Play continues in the same manner as in Four-hand Cribbage. Care must be taken in scoring the peg and hands, since so many cards are involved.

Cribbage Solitaire

Jake the snake has taken a vacation to Hawaii, paid for by his Cribbage winnings, and has left you with the "Cribbage withdrawals." What do you do with the daily hour or so usually spent playing Cribbage with Jake? Why, play Cribbage Solitaire!

This game is simple, fast, and difficult to win. . .but it can be done.

Cribbage Solitaire consists of six hands and six Cribs. In addition, you peg your six hands.

To begin, deal two cards down to form part of your hand. Then one down to form part of the Crib. Deal two more to your hand, one more to the Crib, and finally two more to your hand (your hand has six cards, the Crib has two).

Of the six cards, discard two to form a four-card Crib. Then *turn the top card* of the deck for the Starter.

Now peg your four-card hand for maximum count. For example, you are holding a 5-10-10-Jack. Play the 5 first. then a 10 for "fifteen-two," another 10 for "twenty-five, a pair and a 'Go.' " The remaining Jack also scores a "Go" for one point. Your peg totals six points.

After scoring the peg, count your hand, then the Crib.

To begin the second deal, the first hand Starter becomes one of the six cards to form your hand. Again deal the Crib two cards. Repeat this process until you complete the game with the sixth deal (the deck will contain four cards after six deals).

If you have played astutely and have had some luck, you can beat old man Solitaire, but it won't be easy. You must average twenty points per deal (plus one) to win this 121-point game.

This game doesn't tax the mind too much and should hold you until Jake returns from Hawaii, all tanned and raring to go.

Player's Name

	Won	Lost		Won	Lost		Won	Lost		Won	Lost		Won	Lost		Won	Lost		Won	Lost		Won	Lost
Pct.			Pct.			Pct.			Pct.			Pct.			Pct.			Pct.			Pct.		

Player's Name

Won	Lost	Won	Lost	Won	Lost	Won	Lost	Won	Lost	Won	Lost	Won	Lost	Won	Lost
Pct.		Pct.		Pct.		Pct.		Pct.		Pct.		Pct.		Pct.	

Player's Name

Won	Lost	Won	Lost	Won	Lost	Won	Lost	Won	Lost	Won	Lost	Won	Lost	Won	Lost
Pct.		Pct.		Pct.		Pct.		Pct.		Pct.		Pct.		Pct.	

Player's Name

Won	Lost	Won	Lost	Won	Lost	Won	Lost	Won	Lost	Won	Lost	Won	Lost	Won	Lost
Pct.		Pct.		Pct.		Pct.		Pct.		Pct.		Pct.		Pct.	

Player's Name

Won	Lost	Won	Lost	Won	Lost	Won	Lost	Won	Lost	Won	Lost	Won	Lost	Won	Lost
Pct.		Pct.		Pct.		Pct.		Pct.		Pct.		Pct.		Pct.	

Player's Name

Won	Lost	Won	Lost	Won	Lost	Won	Lost	Won	Lost	Won	Lost	Won	Lost	Won	Lost
Pct.		Pct.		Pct.		Pct.		Pct.		Pct.		Pct.		Pct.	

Player's Name

Won	Lost	Won	Lost	Won	Lost	Won	Lost	Won	Lost	Won	Lost	Won	Lost	Won	Lost
Pct.		Pct.		Pct.		Pct.		Pct.		Pct.		Pct.		Pct.	

Player's Name

Won	Lost	Won	Lost	Won	Lost	Won	Lost	Won	Lost	Won	Lost	Won	Lost	Won	Lost
Pct.		Pct.		Pct.		Pct.		Pct.		Pct.		Pct.		Pct.	

Player's Name

Won	Lost	Won	Lost	Won	Lost	Won	Lost	Won	Lost	Won	Lost	Won	Lost	Won	Lost
Pct.		Pct.		Pct.		Pct.		Pct.		Pct.		Pct.		Pct.	

Player's Name

Won	Lost	Won	Lost	Won	Lost	Won	Lost	Won	Lost	Won	Lost	Won	Lost	Won	Lost
Pct.		Pct.		Pct.		Pct.		Pct.		Pct.		Pct.		Pct.	

Player's Name

Won	Lost	Won	Lost	Won	Lost	Won	Lost	Won	Lost	Won	Lost	Won	Lost	Won	Lost
Pct.		Pct.		Pct.		Pct.		Pct.		Pct.		Pct.		Pct.	

Player's Name

Won	Lost	Won	Lost	Won	Lost	Won	Lost	Won	Lost	Won	Lost	Won	Lost	Won	Lost
Pct.		Pct.		Pct.		Pct.		Pct.		Pct.		Pct.		Pct.	

Player's Name

Won	Lost	Won	Lost	Won	Lost	Won	Lost	Won	Lost	Won	Lost	Won	Lost	Won	Lost
Pct.		Pct.		Pct.		Pct.		Pct.		Pct.		Pct.		Pct.	

Player's Name

Won	Lost	Won	Lost	Won	Lost	Won	Lost	Won	Lost	Won	Lost	Won	Lost	Won	Lost
Pct.		Pct.		Pct.		Pct.		Pct.		Pct.		Pct.		Pct.	